DRAFTING TORCHON LACE PATTERNS

Alexandra Stillwell

Dryad Press Ltd   London

NORTH
CIRC
HANDICRAFTS

ACKNOWLEDGMENT

◀ *Frontispiece (overleaf)*
A freestyle fan made on the pricking
featured in figures 179 A-C

Thanks must go to all my students who have worked at pattern making, confirmed my belief in its merit and encouraged me to write this book. Thanks also to Vi Bullard, Sue Warburton, Eunice Kirk, Ginny Kennedy and Maureen Brazier who have allowed me to use their ideas; to Joan Savage, Vi Bullard, Debbie Moller, Jill Smoothy, and Luton Museum for use of their material, to Alan Meek ABIPP for taking the photographs and to Octopus Books Limited for allowing me to reproduce their sketch of an Edwardian lady. I am particularly grateful to Sue Wise who worked from my notes and checked that the instructions are intelligible, Irene Munro who helped me check the script and Janet McGill who translated my scrawl into a typewritten script.

© Alexandra Stillwell 1986
First published 1986
Reprinted 1992

Typeset by Tek-Art Ltd, Kent
printed in Gt Britain by
The Bath Press Ltd
Bath, Avon
for the publishers
B.T. Batsford Ltd
4 Fitzhardinge Street
London W1H 0AH

ISBN 0 7134 7197 2

CONTENTS

Introduction   7

1   **Drawing Materials**   9
Graph paper
Drawing aids

2   **The Fan Pattern**   11
Footside
Torchon ground
Fan boundary
Points along the curve
Corners – three variations
Use of different stitches

3   **Fan Pattern
    Variations**   18
Straight-edged fan
Inward-curving fan
Heart-shaped fan
Double fan
Trail edge

4   **Spanish or
    Fir Tree Fan**   23
Plotting the corner
Spanish fan variation
Feather

5   **Scallop Fan and
    French Fan**   32

6   **Borders**   36
Plain
Pea
Large pea
German spider
Scallop
Decorated fans
and borders
Plaited decoration
Fringe

7   **Motifs within the Ground
    and Copying Patterns**   47
Diamonds
Triangles
Hearts
Trails
Spiders
Tallies
Gimps
Fillings

8   **Changing Scale**   62
Different scales of
graph paper
Plotting diagonally
across the paper
Thread chart

9   **Adapting Patterns**   70
Corners and side reverse
Paperweights

Brooches
Square mats
Rectangular mats
Bookmarks and insertions
Items made in several
pieces

10   **Freestyle Pictures**   106
Edwardian lady
Toadstools

11   **Circular Lace**   113
Narrow circular edging
Working out grids
Wider edgings
Circular mat
Collar
Freestyle fan

12   **Ovals and Ellipses**   126
Simple oval edging
An ellipse

13   **Making a Pricking**   133
Repeating pattern
Dovetailing
Fitting a pattern on a roller

Appendix – grids   137
Suppliers   143
Further reading   143
Index   144

Introduction

Traditionally lace patterns were designed by the few trained designers and supplied by lace dealers and teachers. The lacemaker would use a pattern, until it became unusable due to the enlargement of holes or tearing. She would then pin a new, transparent, piece of parchment over the original and prick through. The exact positions of the original holes within the now enlarged spaces would be difficult to find and the positions of the newly pricked holes would vary from the original. After repeated repricking the arrangement of the holes would become very irregular (figure 1). Since lace threads are held in position by pins and the position of the pins depends on their pinholes, lace will show the same irregularities as its pricking. Accurate lace can only be made on an accurate pricking. Even today many lacemakers prick through patterns to make a copy, not only of the design but the errors also!

Some photostat machines distort patterns by making them narrower without changing the length. When a pattern has been recopied several times the distortion becomes quite marked. This is one reason why it is often impossible to match four photostats to make a square border or relocate lace onto its pricking when 'moving up' after turning a corner. The best way to ensure good lace is to draft the pricking oneself. First class lace cannot be made on a second class pricking.

Pattern drafting is time-consuming and frequently exasperating, but it is very rewarding and has many advantages over other methods of copying. Apart from the production of accurate patterns the actual drawing of the pattern gives an idea of the structure of the lace it will produce and hence, an insight into its making.

A pattern maker can also change the scale of the pattern to match a coarser or finer thread to make lace suitable for a table-cloth or handkerchief. She will be able to design corners, copy from patterns and adapt designs for use as edgings, insertions, mats and paperweight designs and, with experience, design her own lace for similar items and make pictures.

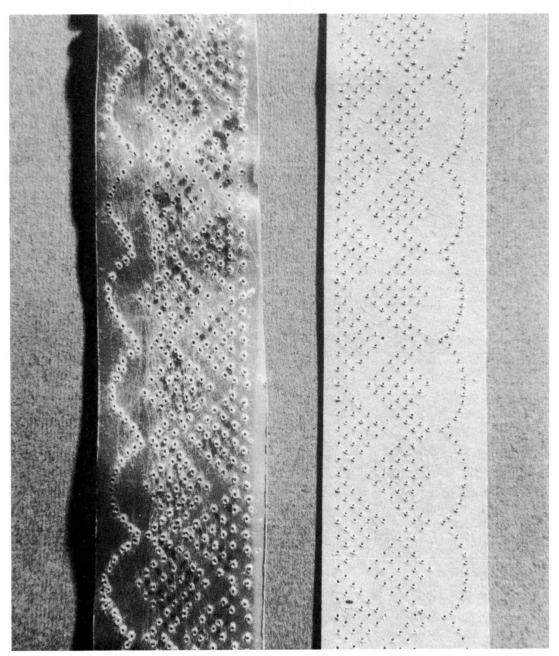

Figure 1.
A Luton Museum pricking showing
distortion probably caused by poor
copying, together with an accurate
pricking

1.
Drawing Materials

GRAPH PAPER

Torchon lace patterns are drafted on graph paper. For a beginner 1/10in squares are the most suitable size although many other sizes can be useful to the lacemaker. Always take a ruler and check the size of the squares when buying, as many shops only stock the 2mm (3/32in) square size. Good quality paper is the best to start on as the tougher the paper, e.g. cartridge, the better it will survive the repeated use of a rubber. The graph squares are also printed on detail paper which is usually the cheapest but rather flimsy to use. Tracing paper is used for graphs as well and can be used when copying but it tends to retain marks easily and mistakes cannot always be completely removed.

The 1/10in (figure 2) and 2mm (figure 3) squared papers used straight or diagonally will provide four scales to work on and can be used to produce lace suitable for most requirements.

Polar co-ordinate (circular) graph paper is very useful when drafting circular mats.

DRAWING AIDS

Use an HB or B pencil, kept sharp. Use it gently and avoid making deep marks that are difficult to remove with an eraser. If a dot cannot be rubbed out draw a ring round it – the lacemakers' symbol for a mistake.

A draughtsman's plastic eraser is worth the investment. The eraser wears away, not the paper!

A radius aid – a template with circular holes and projections – is very useful for drawing in the curves for fans. However, buttons, coins or any similar articles are suitable. Sometimes compasses can be used if the fan has a shallow curve and some like to use French curves.

A transparent acetate sheet (0.007in) is invaluable for repeating curves along the edge of a pattern and for pricking repeats for a long pattern; its straight edge or a transparent ruler is useful for lining up holes when copying from a pattern or piece of lace.

For convenience many of the pieces of lace were worked in DMC Retors d'Alsace No.30 on patterns drawn diagonally across 1/10in, (2.5mm) graph paper.

Figure 2.
1/10in (2.5mm) graph paper

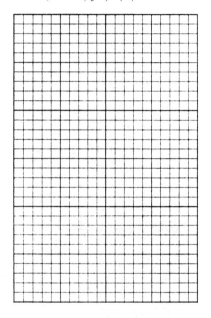

Figure 3.
2mm graph paper

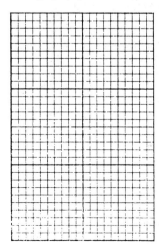

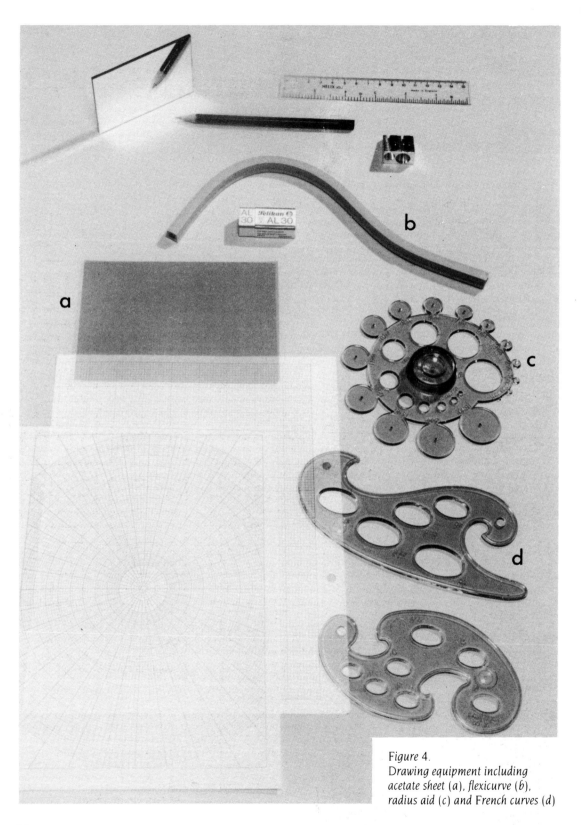

Figure 4.
Drawing equipment including
acetate sheet (a), flexicurve (b),
radius aid (c) and French curves (d)

2.
The Fan Pattern

This fan pattern is usually one of the first to be tackled by a beginner and uses many basic techniques. The numerical sequence indicated only applies to the plotting of the pattern, and is not suitable for making the lace. It is also one of many sequences since the points can be plotted in any order.

Start drawing the pattern by plotting the footpins *1-10* on alternate horizontal lines working down the paper. Continue for about 10cm (4in) (figure 7).

Figure 5.
The basic fan

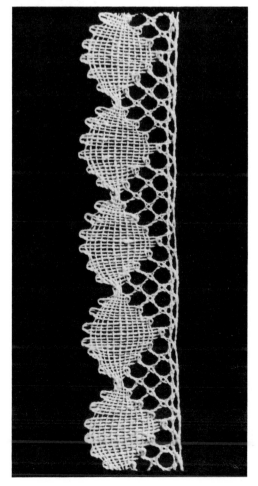

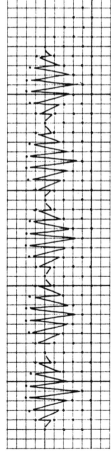

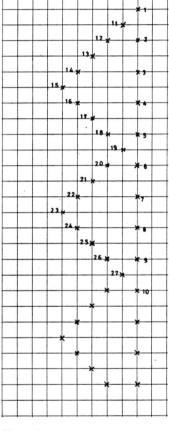

Figure 7.
Plotting the footside and zig-zag border of the torchon ground

◀ *Figure 6.*
The basic fan (pricking).

FOOTSIDE

Mark the points *11-15* along an imaginary diagonal line joining the corners of the squares starting from point *1*. Work along the diagonal that starts at point *15* and slopes downwards towards the foot, i.e. linking points *15-6*, mark points *16-19*. Work along the next diagonal towards the head that starts with points *5* and *9* marking points *20-23*; then back along the one ending at point *10* marking points *24-27*. Continue this zig-zag for the length of the footside. These pinholes form the inner boundary of the fans (figure 7).

TORCHON GROUND

Plot the torchon ground between this zig-zag line of points and the footside, starting with three points along the diagonal linking points *2* and *16*, i.e. points *28-30*, two between points *3* and *17* – points *31* and *32*, and one between points *4* and *18* – point *33*. Plot the torchon ground between the zig-zag and the footside for the length of the pattern (figure 8).

These points make triangular sections of ground showing the typical pattern of points, i.e. a diamond lattice arrangement.

Figure 8.
Plotting torchon ground

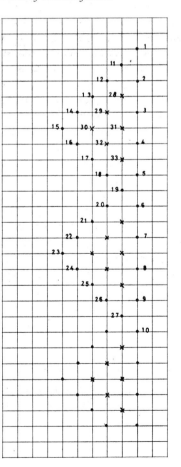

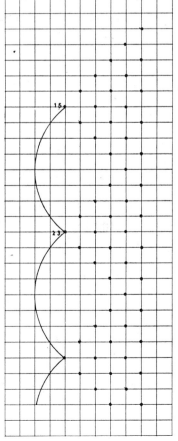

◀ *Figure 9.*
Drawing curves for the fans

Figure 10.
Lines to assist drawing a curve freehand
▼

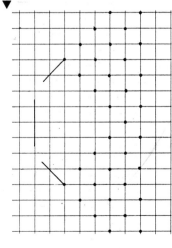

FAN BOUNDARY

Next draw the curve at the head of the fan between points *15* and *23* using a radius aid, coin, French curves or in free-hand. The widest portion of the fan reaches the second vertical line to the left of the one connecting points *15* and *23* (figure 9).

When drawing the curve free-hand it helps if the diagonals that extend outward from points *1-15* and *10-23* are lightly sketched in together with a vertical line where the fan is at its widest. Draw the curve so that it fits between these lines (figure 10).

POINTS ALONG THE CURVE

Six points *A-F* are drawn along the curve so that they are equi-distant from each other and points *15* and *23* (figure 11). If the guideline is drawn now it helps the spacing of the six points and checks that the correct number has been plotted. As it is very tedious to keep drawing curves and plotting the points, as well as being impossible to keep the six points in identical places for all the fans, there is a short cut.

After drawing the curve for the first fan and carefully spacing the six points *A-F* along it, place a piece of acetate over the curve and attach to the pattern by inserting pins at points *15* and *23*. (Collect pieces of acetate from shirt packing, handkerchief box fronts, etc.) Prick through points *A-F*. Remove the pins and place the acetate pricking across the next 'V' of the zig-zag and insert pins through points *23* and *P* prick *A-F*, then pass on to the next 'V' (figure 11).

Always draw the line that indicates the path of the workers when the lace is made. This is the final check that there is the correct number of pins along the headside. It is also an aid to working the lace and helps the pattern bear some resemblance to the lace that will be made on it. Guidelines drawn on patterns usually follow standard routes but as patterns are very personal the lacemaker can add any other lines and hieroglyphics that will help with the making of the lace – to the consternation of anyone else trying to follow it! This and the following patterns can be worked in any of the threads listed in the section '¹⁄₁₀in graph paper (straight)' of the thread chart. Torchon lace can be very attractive when worked with a fine thread; the pattern being drawn on a smaller scale, see chapter 8. Alternatively the size of a pattern can be reduced using a photocopying machine.

CORNERS – THREE VARIATIONS

Corners for torchon lace pose few problems (figures 12 and 13). For the fan pattern finish the length of pattern with the points corresponding to numbers *5, 19-23*. Then mark points

Figure 11.
Plotting points along the curve

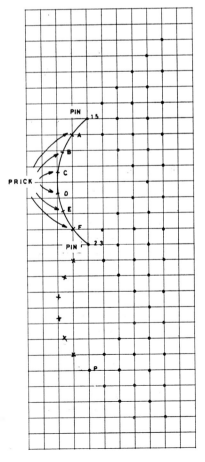

Figure 12.
A corner for the basic fan

Figure 13.
A corner for the basic fan (pricking)

Figure 14.
Plotting the points at the corner

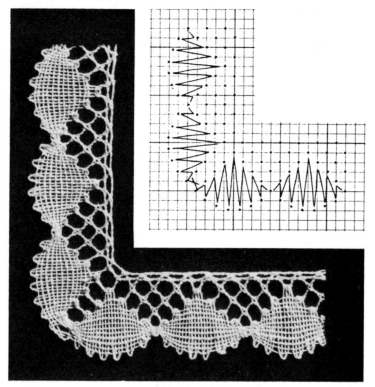

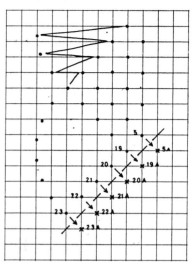

5A, 19A-23A diagonally across the squares through the corner (figure 14) and continue with the zig-zag line starting from these points. Draw the footside for the new section at right angles to the first section of footside starting from 5A and plot the ground. Use the template to mark the points along the curves of the fans (figure 15).

Figure 15.
Plotting the fan 'around the corner'

Many lacemakers do not like this corner as the workers must be changed. The next corner improves on this (figures 16 and 17). A point is placed at *G* – the workers follow the guideline on the pattern.

The footside can also be varied by placing point *H* in the corner (figure 18).

Figure 16.
An alternative corner for the basic fan

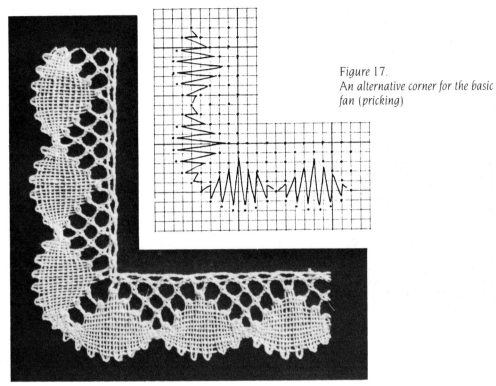

Figure 17.
An alternative corner for the basic fan (pricking)

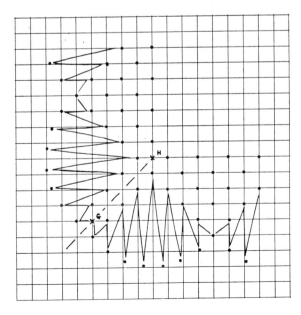

Figure 18.
Plotting the alternative corner for the basic fan

The third variation of the corner has a pin at the central point of the curve around the corner (figures 19 and 20). Prepare this corner by plotting the basic corner, then erase the two fan points *23* and *23A* adjacent to the broken line through the corner (figure 21). Replace these two with a single point *R* between them (figure 22). As this leaves large gaps between *R* and *F*, and *FA* erase *F* and *FA* replacing them with *S* and *T* (figure 23). The worker follows the guideline on the pattern.

USE OF DIFFERENT STITCHES
The pricking is only half the story when working or designing a piece of lace; the effectiveness of the design is determined by the choice and balance of the stitches used. Always place a light airy stitch or ground against one that is substantially more solid. Two areas of similar density next to each other provide little contrast and the design will lose its impact.

Figure 20.
A *third corner for the basic fan*
(*pricking*)

Figure 19.
A *third corner for the basic fan* ▶

Figure 21.
Plotting *the third corner for the basic fan*
▼

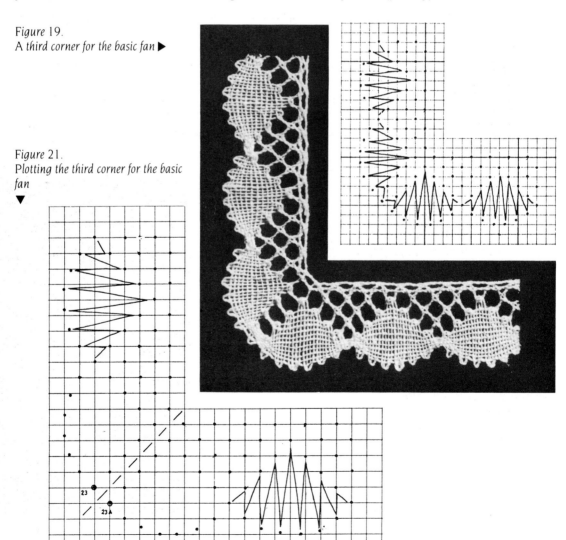

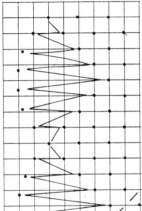

Figure 22.
Plotting the centre point of the third corner for the basic fan

Figure 23.
Adjusting the points of the third corner for the basic fan

Figure 24 shows some stitches and grounds used on the fan pattern pricking with the third corner. All were made in the same thread and no pinholes were added or ignored.

Figure 24.
Lace made on the basic fan pattern
(a) Whole stitch fan, torchon ground
(b) Half stitch fan with whole stitch and twist edge, twisted half stitch torchon ground
(c) Whole stitch fan with twisted workers near the edge, whole stitch torchon ground
(d) Whole stitch fan with whole stitch and twist edge, rose ground
(e) Half stitch fan with whole stitch and twist edge, closed check ground ▶

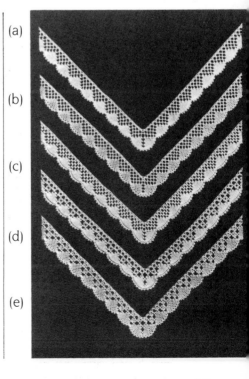

(a)

(b)

(c)

(d)

(e)

3.
Fan Pattern Variations

Try altering the fan pattern, draw a smaller fan and add points along the footside to make the lace wider. If the pattern is made wider the fan can be made larger by increasing the number of points along each diagonal of its inner boundary. Changing the size of the fan will mean that the number of points along the curve will change. There is always one less point along the curve points *A-F* than along

Figure 25.
Variations on the fan
(a) A straight-edged fan
(b) An inward curving fan
(c) A heart-shaped fan with a
division of twisted passives
(d) A double fan
(e) A double fan with single fans at
the corner
(f) A trail edge
(g) A trail edge with twisted passive
division and an alternative corner

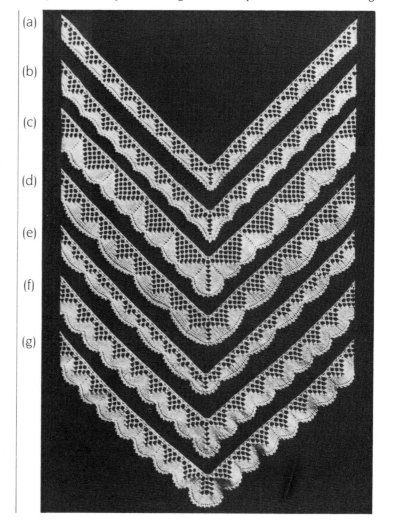

(a)

(b)

(c)

(d)

(e)

(f)

(g)

the diagonals of the inner boundary of the fan points *15-19-23*. The guideline will check that the correct number of points has been plotted – if the worker cannot be drawn, adjust the number of points along the fan.

STRAIGHT-EDGED FAN

Points *A-F* may be placed along the line connecting points *15* and *23* (figures 25 and 26). For this fan the basic corner may be used; an improved corner will require one extra point on the outer edge *G*, pinholes *23* and *23A* adjusted to even the spacing, and two extra points *H* and *J* (figure 27).

Figure 28.
The inward curving fan (pricking)

Figure 26.
The straight-edged fan (pricking)

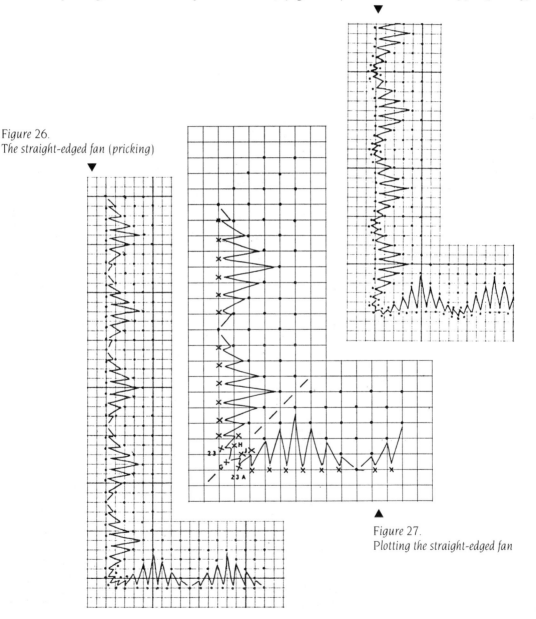

Figure 27.
Plotting the straight-edged fan

19

INWARD-CURVING FAN

The outer edge may curve inwards (figures 25 and 28). In this case point *15* is removed and replaced by points *M* and *N* and an extra point *P* one square away from them. The corner also requires special treatment. An extra hole *Q* will be required between points *P* and *PA* which will need adjusting to produce a good curve. To balance this, two extra holes will be needed at *S* and *T* (figure 29).

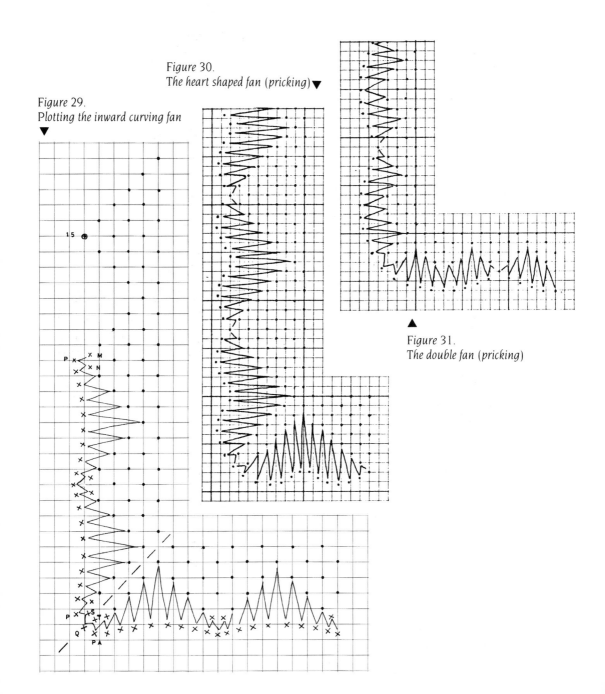

Figure 30.
The heart shaped fan (pricking)▼

Figure 29.
Plotting the inward curving fan
▼

▲

Figure 31.
The double fan (pricking)

HEART-SHAPED FAN

When the fan is larger the single curve can be replaced by two smaller curves (figures 25 and 30). This results in a heart-shaped fan. Note that there are two level pinholes in the 'dip'.

Figure 34.
The trail edge with two holes at the 'dip' and an alternative corner
▼

Figure 32.
The double fan with single fans at the corner (pricking)
▼

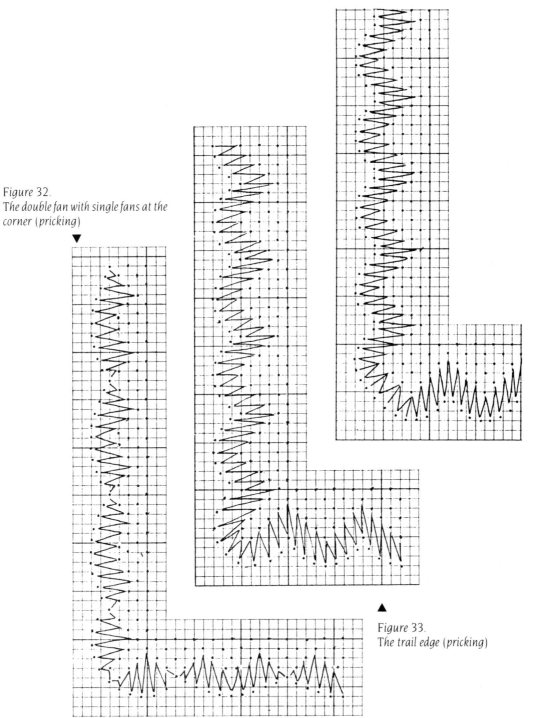

▲
Figure 33.
The trail edge (pricking)

21

DOUBLE FAN

On the other hand the curves of two fans can be replaced by a single larger curve (figures 25 and 31). Two corners can be formed from this fan, either the corner is bounded by two complete double fans or two basic fans can be fitted, one on either side (figures 25 and 32).

TRAIL EDGE

The curve of the head pins can follow the zig-zag boundary of the ground, resulting in a wavy trail along the edge. This can be drawn in two ways, either with one point in the 'dip' between the curves (figures 25 and 33) or with two points (figures 25 and 34). In each case the points are evenly spaced along the curve. For the latter, the corner has been drawn with two lines of torchon ground between the two 'V's of the trail. No extra pinholes have been introduced along the inner edge of the trail to balance those along the outer edge, instead back stitches have been worked as indicated by the guideline on the pattern.

Summary

All the variations can be drawn following the same order of work as the original fan, i.e.:

(i) plot the footside; (ii) plot the inner zig-zag boundary of the fans; (iii) plot the torchon ground between the zig-zag and the footside; (iv) draw the curve of the headside; (v) plot the points, equally spaced, along one curve of the fan; (vi) draw the line of the workers to check that there is the correct number of holes along the curve; (vii) prepare a transparent template of the headside pins; and (viii) use the template to mark the holes along the remaining fans.

Remember that the pattern you prepare is yours and it may be modified as you wish. These patterns and instructions are the basis of the work but curves may be changed and pinholes moved, introduced or removed providing that the lace, when made, looks good.

All these variations on the fan have been worked in whole stitch, with the workers twisted between the two edge pairs of passives. The heart-shaped fan and one of the trails have the passives twisted to make divisions.

All may be worked in whole stitch, half stitch, or whole stitch with the worker, passives, or both twisted at selected places. The choice of stitch for the fans depends on the ground to be used or vice versa. Always keep the contrast of an open, airy stitch against one that is more solid.

4.
The Spanish or Fir Tree Fan

Figure 35.

The Spanish or fir tree fan

(a) Fan workers of the same thread as the rest of the lace

(b) Fan workers wound double with the same thread as the rest of the lace

(c) Fan workers of a heavier thread than the rest of the lace

(d) The workers of the fan replaced by a thick gimp ▶

There are two basic variations of the Spanish or fir tree fan and several ways of working them. In the most usual form of the fan the worker is taken to the point of the fan at the half-way stage; in the other it is taken to the head. The fan can be worked in whole stitch and twist or plain whole stitch with a

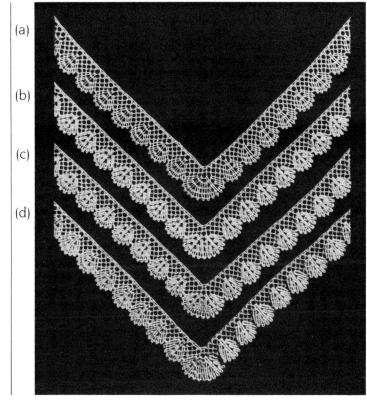

(a)

(b)

(c)

(d)

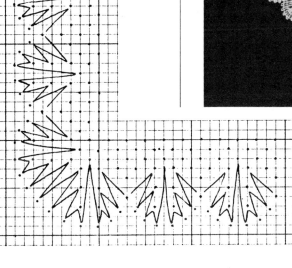

Figure 36.
The Spanish or fir tree fan (pricking)

23

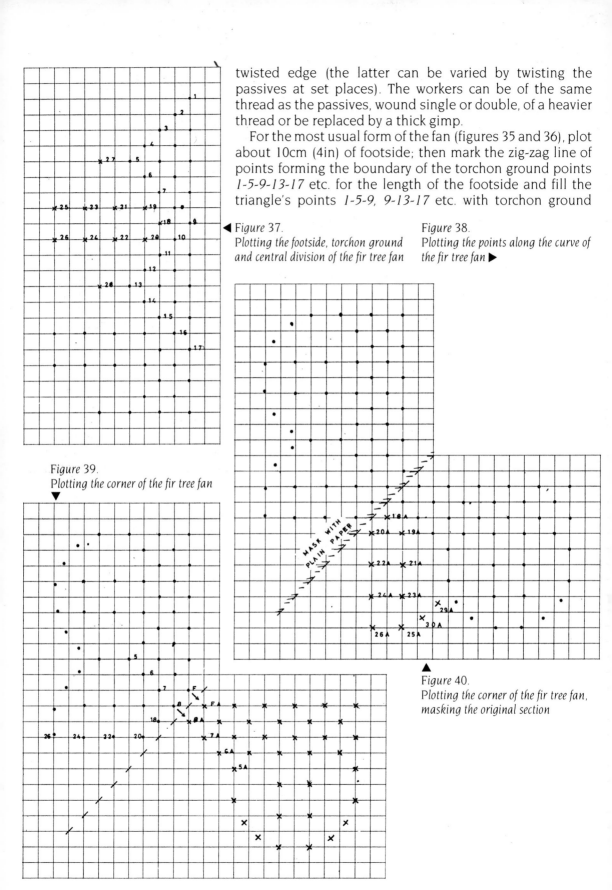

twisted edge (the latter can be varied by twisting the passives at set places). The workers can be of the same thread as the passives, wound single or double, of a heavier thread or be replaced by a thick gimp.

For the most usual form of the fan (figures 35 and 36), plot about 10cm (4in) of footside; then mark the zig-zag line of points forming the boundary of the torchon ground points *1-5-9-13-17* etc. for the length of the footside and fill the triangle's points *1-5-9, 9-13-17* etc. with torchon ground

◀ Figure 37.
Plotting the footside, torchon ground and central division of the fir tree fan

Figure 38.
Plotting the points along the curve of the fir tree fan ▶

Figure 39.
Plotting the corner of the fir tree fan
▼

MASK WITH PLAIN PAPER

▲
Figure 40.
Plotting the corner of the fir tree fan, masking the original section

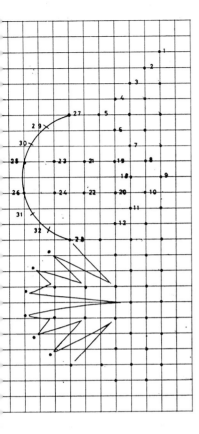

figure 37). (These points have not been numbered in the diagram.) Next plot the points for the central division of the fan; point *18* diagonally to the left of and below point *8* and the pairs of points *19* and *20*, *21* and *22*, *23* and *24* and *25* and *26* extending outwards towards the head. Now mark the low points between the fans – points *27* and *28* (figure 37). So far all these points fit into the torchon ground pattern namely – when marking diagonally across the squares a point is made at every intersection whereas, when progressing horizontally or vertically along the lines, points are only made at alternate intersections.

The curve of the fan extends from point *27* to *28* passing through points *25* and *26*; then put in points *29* and *30* so that they are equally spaced between points *27* and *25* and points *31* and *32* between points *26* and *28* (figure 38). Make a transparent template of the points along the curve and use it to prick the points along the curves of the remaining fans. Finally draw the guide lines.

PLOTTING THE CORNER

Plot the above pattern as far as points *8*, *18*, *20*, *22*, *24*, *26* and the footside point *F* (figure 39). Mark points *FA* and *8A* diagonally opposite points *F* and *8* and plot the footside of the new section, at right angles to the first section, starting from point *FA*. Continue by plotting points *8A-5A* along the extension of the line through points *5-8*. This is the beginning of the zig-zag of the new section, continue it for the length of the footside. Plot the torchon ground within the triangles and complete the fans along the new section. Most of the confusion experienced when drawing these corners is caused by trying to visualise the complete corner whilst plotting it. To avoid this, mask the original section with a piece of plain paper (figure 40). Work on the new section, marking points *18A-26A* by direct comparison with the fans along the new section. *Use the transparent template to position points *29A* and *30A*. Remove the masking paper and draw the curve from point *26-26A*.

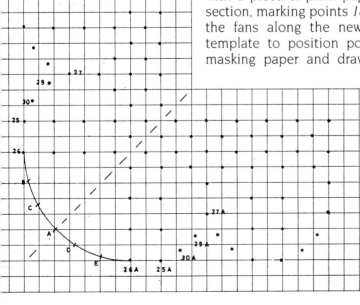

◀ *Figure 41.*
Plotting the points along the corner curve of the fir tree fan

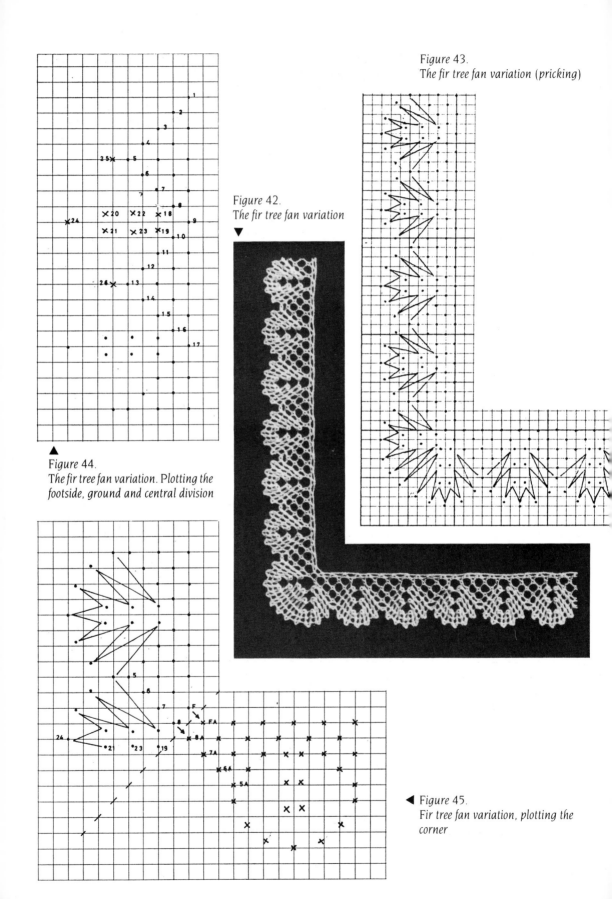

Figure 43.
The fir tree fan variation (pricking)

Figure 42.
The fir tree fan variation
▼

▲
Figure 44.
The fir tree fan variation. Plotting the
footside, ground and central division

◀ Figure 45.
Fir tree fan variation, plotting the
corner

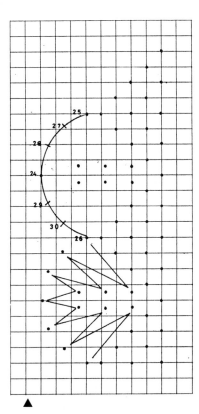

Position point *A* at the centre of the curve points *B* and *C* equally spaced between points *26* and *A*, and *D* and *E* between points *A* and *26A* (figure 41). It is sometimes easier to work as far as * and draw the complete curve points *27-27A* passing through points *25, 26, 26A* and *25A*. Points *26* and *26A* may be 'moved' to make the spacing even. finish by marking the guidelines.

SPANISH FAN VARIATION (figures 42 and 43)
Start plotting as for the Spanish fan described above. Begin the footside at point *1*, mark the zig-zag, points *1-5-9-13-17* etc. and the torchon ground filling the triangles (figure 44). If the pairs of points *18* and *19*, *20* and *21* and *22* and *23* extending towards the head are plotted in the same positions as the basic Spanish fan there will be a gap at the

▲
Figure 46.
Fir tree fan variation, plotting the points along the curve

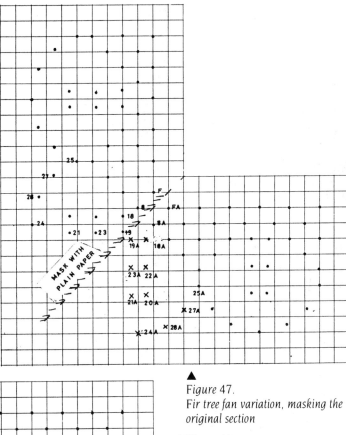

▲
Figure 47.
Fir tree fan variation, masking the original section

◀ Figure 48.
Fir tree fan variation, plotting points along the corner curve

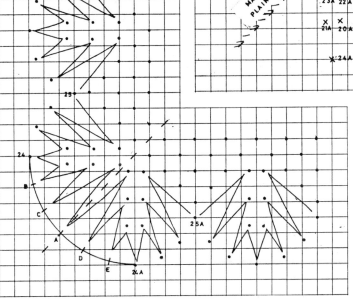

27

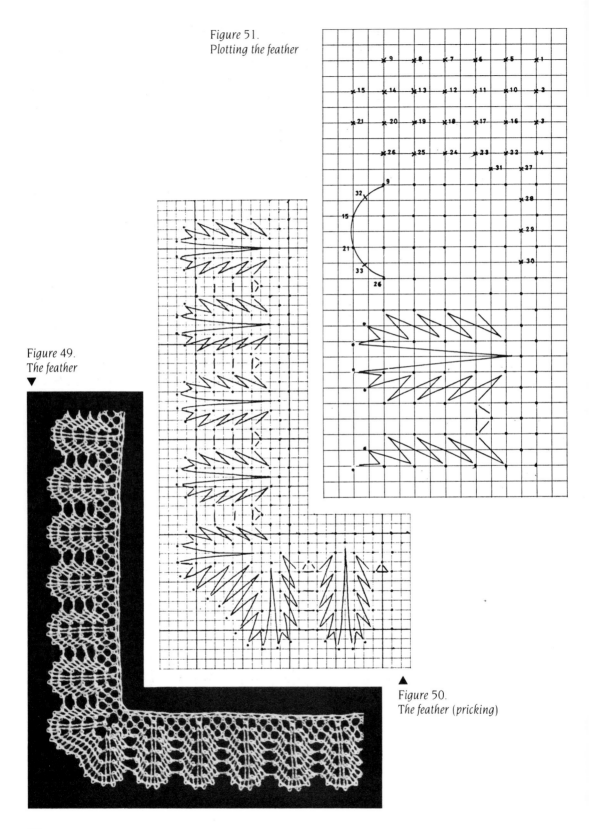

Figure 51.
Plotting the feather

Figure 49.
The feather
▼

Figure 50.
The feather (pricking)

28

centre of the fan and an ugly hole at its point. To avoid this the points are 'moved' towards each other and towards the point of the fan. Plot points *18* and *19* midway on the lines, points *20* and *21* in the centres of the squares, then points *22* and *23* mid-way between the two pairs *18* and *19*, and *20* and *21*. The central point of the curve *24* is marked next. Since the pairs of points have been 'moved' the whole fan has been reduced in depth, hence the low points *25* and *26* between the fans must be 'moved' a little closer towards the torchon ground.

Draw the curve from point *25* to *26* through point *24* and position two points *27* and *28* between points *25* and *24*, and points *29* and *30* between points *24* and *26* (figure 45). Draw the guide lines.

The corner for this fan is tackled as for the basic Spanish fan – plot the above pattern as far as points *8, 19, 23, 21* and *24* and the footside point *F* (figure 46). Mark points *FA* and *8A* diagonally opposite points *F* and *8* and plot the footside of the new section, at right angles to the first section, starting from point *FA*. Continue by plotting points *8A-5A* along the extension of the line through points *5-8* and continue with the zig-zag of points as required. Complete the torchon ground and the fans for the new section. Mask

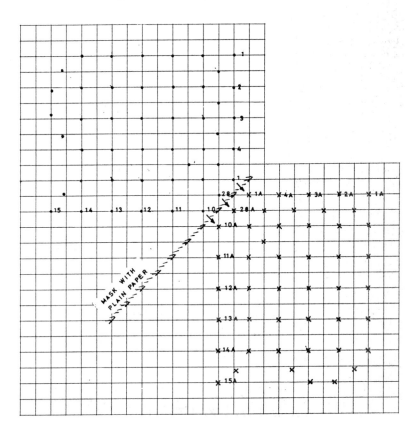

Figure 52.
The feather, plotting the corner

the original section with a piece of plain paper and mark points *18A-24A* by direct comparison with the fans along the new section (figure 47). Points *27A* and *28A* may be put in now using the transparent template, or after drawing the full curve. Remove the masking paper and draw the curve between points *24* and *24A* or from point *25* to *25A* passing through points *24* and *24A* (figure 48). Plot point *A* at the centre of the curve then two points *B* and *C* equally spaced between points *24* and *A*, and two points *D* and *E* between points *A* and *24A*. Draw the guidelines.

FEATHER (figures 49 and 50)
The Feather is an elongated version of the Spanish fan. Start by plotting the footside down the paper, points *1-4* etc. From point *1* plot five points *5-9* horizontally along the row, remembering that alternate intersections only are used (figure 51). Plot six points *10-15* across the paper from point *2*, six points *16-21* from point *3* and five points *22-26* from point *4*. Repeat these four rows for the length of the footside. Next plot the remaining torchon ground points *27-30* etc., between the footside and the next row, and then one more point *31* on the third line from the footside between the two short rows of points. Draw the curve from point *9* to *26* passing through points *15* and *21*. Add two more points *32* and *33* along the curve, one between points *9* and *15* and the other between points *21* and *26*. Make a transparent template and prick the remaining points for the rest of the fans. Draw the guidelines.

Since this fan is deep, a corner designed along the lines previously described would look ungainly. This time the pairs of points extending outwards at the corner have been 'pushed' closer together and one row 'shortened'. Plot the feather pattern as far as points *1, 28, 10* and *11-15* (figure 52). Mark points *1A, 28A* and *10A* diagonally opposite points *1, 28* and *10*. Starting at point *1A* plot the footside at right angles to the first section. Mask the first section with plain paper as far as the line of dashes through the corner. From point *1A* plot five points towards the head, from point *4A* five points and from points *3A* and *2A* six points. Repeat these four lines for the length of the footside and plot the remaining points to complete the torchon ground and the curves as before. Plot points *10A-15A* and the next lines towards the centre of the corner consisting of only five points *17A-21A* (figure 53). Remove the masking paper and plot points *17* to *21*. Draw the curve for the corner. As fans become deeper the plain curved corner becames unwieldy. This corner has been drawn with an indented curve to add interest. Mark point *A*, the point of the indentation at the

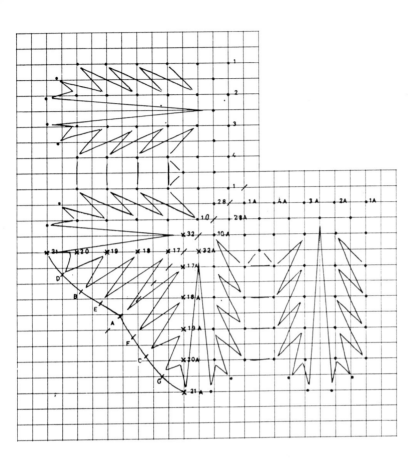

centre of the curve, points *B* and *C* half-way between point *A* and points *21* and *21A* respectively, then points *D-G*, one in each gap. Draw the guidelines. Whenever there is an odd number of points to be marked with equal spacing, put the centre one in first. If there is an odd number left for each side mark the centre one, and so on until all have been positioned or until an even number remains. It is often necessary to correct the spacing several times.

Figure 53.
The feather, plotting points along the corner curve

5.
Scallop Fan and French Fan

SCALLOP (CORONET) FAN (figures 54 and 55)
This fan is placed in a 'V'-shaped space in the torchon ground. Start by plotting about 10cm (4in) of footside down the paper starting from point *1*; mark the zig-zag of points *1-5-9-13-17*, etc. (figure 56). Fill the triangles with torchon ground. (These points have not been numbered in the

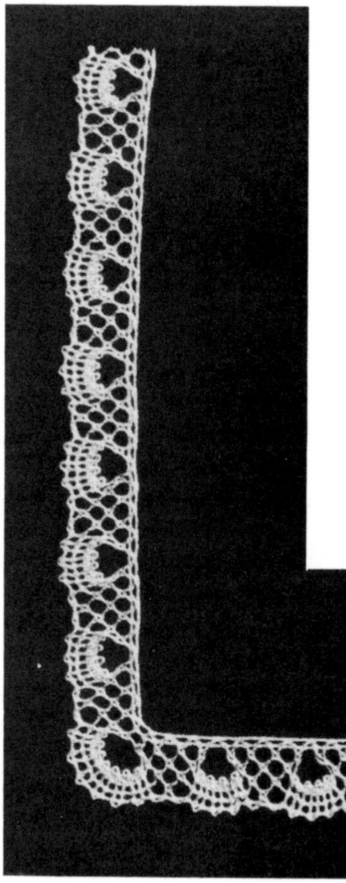

Figure 54.
The scallop or coronet fan ▶

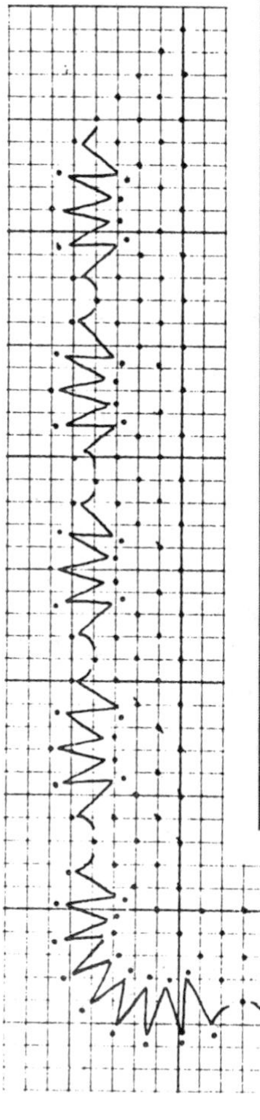

Figure 55.
The scallop or coronet fan (pricking)
▼

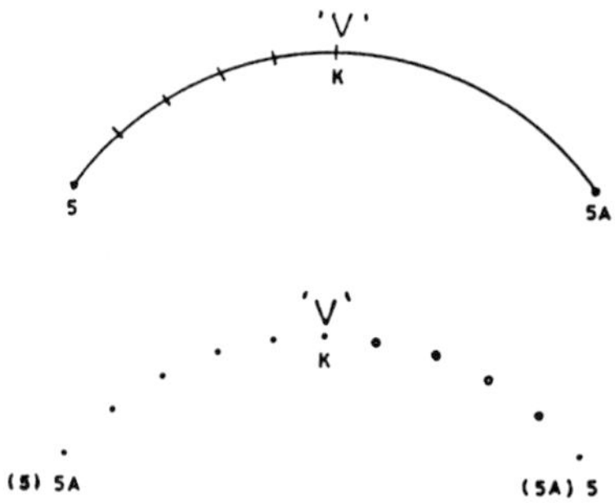

Figure 58.
Plotting points along a curve
▼

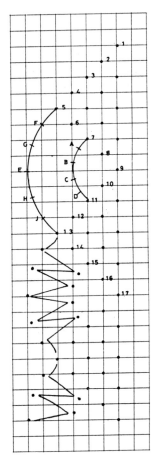

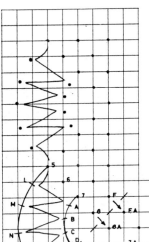

Figure 56.
Plotting the coronet corner

diagram.) Draw the inner curve between points 7 and 11 with the widest part reaching the next vertical line to the left of the one connecting those points. Mark four points A-D evenly spaced between the ends of the curve. Draw the outer curve between points 5 and 13 extending as far as the second vertical line to the left of the one joining these points. Point E lies at the centre of this curve, points F and G are evenly spaced between points 5 and E, and points H and I between points E and 13. A transparent template can be made of these points and used to position the points of the curves for the remaining fans.

To plot the corner finish the footside and ground at points F and 8 (figure 57). Continue marking along the diagonal, points 5-8, adding another four points 8A-5A, these being the corresponding points of the 'other half' of the corner. Mark the first footside point FA of the new section diagonally across the square from point F. Continue plotting the footside for the new section at right angles to the original section, the zig-zag of points forming the inner border of the fan and the torchon ground and the fans. Draw the inner curve between points 7 and 7A and the outer curve between points 5 and 5A so that they extend as far as the corresponding curves of the straight sections on both sides. Mark eight equally spaced points A-E, G, H and I along the inner curve, a central point K on the outer curve, four points L, M, N and P equally spaced between 5 and K and four points Q-T between points K and 5A. Draw the guideline which also checks that the correct number of points has been plotted.

When plotting more than five points along a curve it often helps if a transparent template is made of half the points plus the point at each end, or one end point and the centre point of the curve (figure 58). If this is turned over the other points of the curve can be pricked. When an end point and the centre point are being used scratch a 'V' to identify the centre point. This must always be placed on the centre of the curve regardless of which 'way up' the template is used. For this pattern prick points 5, 5A and K and the four carefully-spaced points between 5 and K. Turn the template over so point 5A is now placed at the original point 5 and vice versa. Point 'V' is at the same place. Prick through the template holes between point K and point 5A to complete the curve.

◀ Figure 57.
Plotting the coronet corner

33

FRENCH (PARIS OR SHELL) FAN (figures 59 and 60)

This fan, usually worked in a combination of whole stitch and whole stitch and twist, can be very effective if coloured workers are used.

Start as usual by plotting about 10cm (4in) of footside starting from point *1*; mark the zig-zag of points forming the boundary of the torchon ground for the length of the zig-zag, points *2-13* etc. and fill the triangles with torchon ground points *14-16* (figure 61). The curve of the fan, between points *5* and *13* extends as far as the second vertical line to the left of these points. Plot six points *A-F* equally spaced along the curve between points *5* and *13*. Finally mark point *17* centrally on the line connecting points *7* and *11*. To plot the corner finish the zig-zag of points at point *8* and the footside

Figure 60.
The French, Paris or shell fan
(pricking) ▼

Figure 61.
Plotting the French, Paris or shell fan ▶

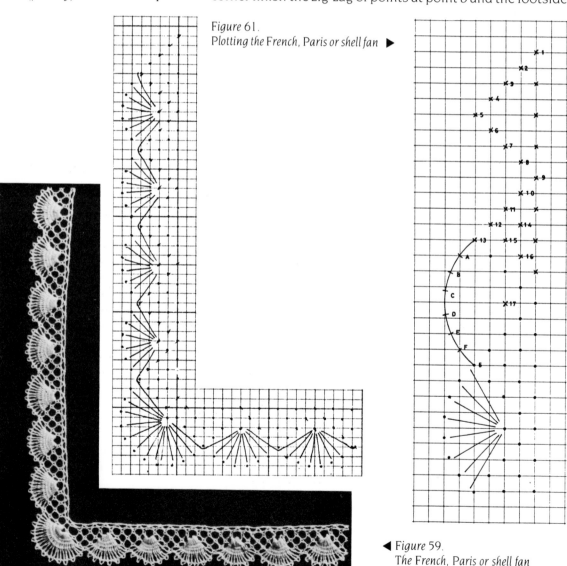

◀ *Figure 59.*
The French, Paris or shell fan

at point *F*. Mark the first footside point *FA* of the new section diagonally across the square from point *F*. Continue the footside for the new section at right angles to the original section (figure 62). Start marking the zig-zag points of the new section by plotting points *8A-5A* along the extension of the line of points *5-8*, then angle it back towards the footside, points *4A-2A*. Continue the zig-zag for the length of the footside, masking the original side as far as the dashed line through the corner if it helps. Fill the triangles with torchon ground and prick the points along the curves of the fans using the transparent template. Mark point *17* for all the fans. Draw the curve for the corner between points *5* and *5A* so that it extends as far as the fans on each side (figure 63). Place 11 points *G-Q*, equally spaced, along this curve. Mark point *18* on the intersection of the lines through points *8* and *8A*. Draw the guide lines. Unlike most other fans the number of points along the curve is relatively independent of the number of points along the zig-zag; the important requirement being the look of the fan when the lace is made.

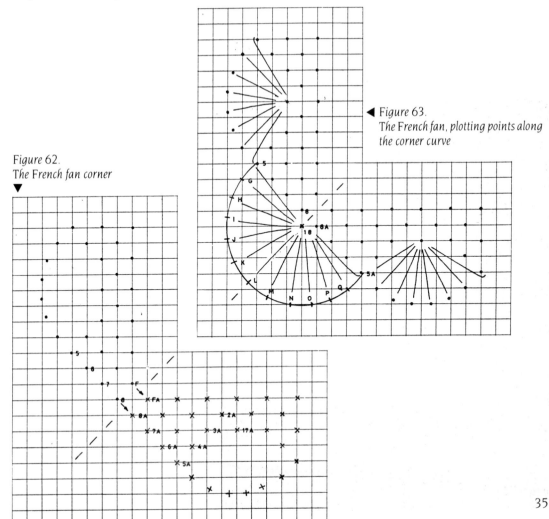

Figure 63.
The French fan, plotting points along the corner curve

Figure 62.
The French fan corner

35

6.
Borders

Apart from fans the headside of torchon lace can be decorated with various borders.

PLAIN (figures 64 and 65)
The plain border is a narrow band of whole stitch worked along the headside of the pattern. It is pricked half as wide again as the usual ground.

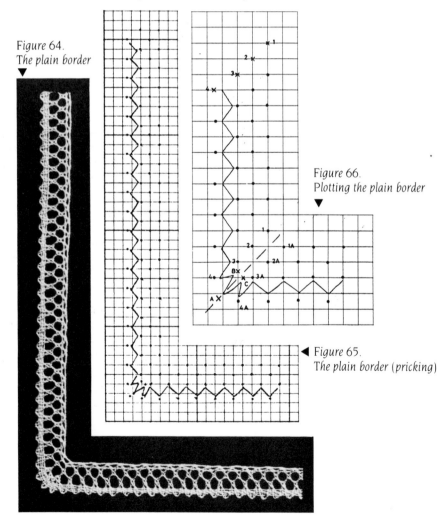

Figure 64.
The plain border
▼

Figure 66.
Plotting the plain border
▼

◀ Figure 65.
The plain border (pricking)

Start from point *1* and plot about 10cm (4in) of footside. Working diagonally plot points *2* and *3*. Point *4* would normally be placed at the next intersection but, since the two plain passive pairs take up more space than this would provide, point *4* is 'moved' outwards by half a square (figure 66). This single line of points constitutes the pattern and should be repeated on alternate lines down the paper. An easy way is to plot the points *2* and *3* repeatedly for the length of the footside. Then mark two points *4* one at each end of the section. Insert a pin through each of these points and hold a ruler firmly against them. Prick the remaining headside points with the pricker held against the ruler.

For the corner plot as far as a line of points *1-4* and mark points *1A-3A* diagonally across the corner squares from points *1-3*. Starting from point *1A* plot the new section of footside at right angles to the original and from points *2A* and *3A* two rows of ground. Plot the headside points *4A* one and a half squares further out as for points *4*. Point *A* is placed between points *4* and *4A* on the diagonal line through the corner, and points *B* and *C* between points *3* and *3A*. Draw the guideline.

PEA (figures 67 and 68)
This decorative border is worked in whole stitch and twist.

Start by plotting points *1* and *2* and continue for about 10cm (4in) of footside. From point *1* plot six points *3-8* diagonally across the paper as for the usual ground (figure 69). From point *2* plot a similar row starting with points *9* and *10*, leaving the next intersection and continuing with points *11-13*. Repeat these two rows as required. Lace worked on this pattern has passives that are slightly wavy; frequently this pattern is drawn with a wider gap between points *4* and *5*. To achieve this 'move' points *5-8* and *11-13* half a square to the left. Lace made on a pattern drawn like this will have straight passives.

For the corner plot the pattern as far as points *2, 9, 10, 11* and *13* and mark five points diagonally across the corner squares from these points, i.e. points *2A, 9A, 10A, 11A* and *13A*. From point *2A* plot the new section of footside at right angles to the original section, then the remaining points to complete the new section. Mark point *A* at the intersection level with points *10* and *10A* and point *B* at the intersection level with points *11* and *11A*. Draw the guidelines.

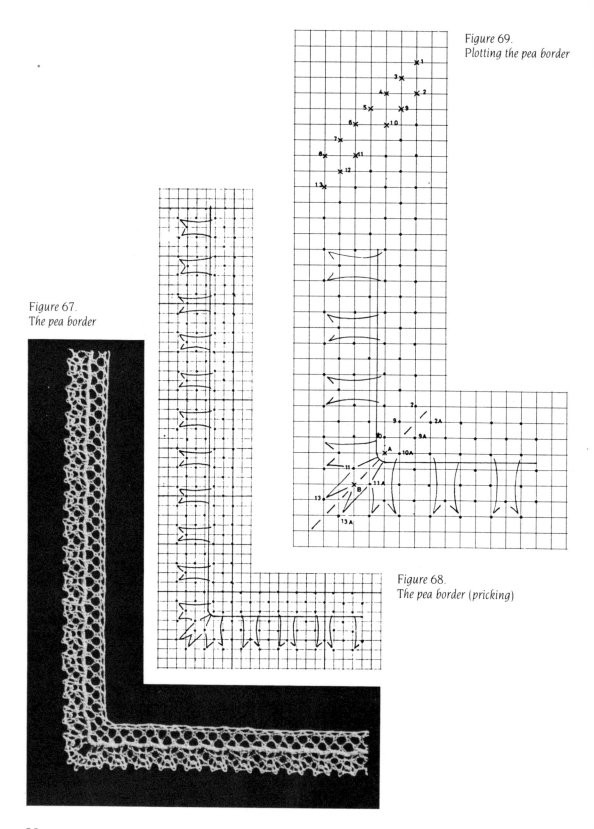

Figure 69.
Plotting the pea border

Figure 67.
The pea border

Figure 68.
The pea border (pricking)

38

LARGE PEA (figures 70 and 71)
This border has been drawn allowing extra space for the two
plain passive pairs. From points *1-3* mark about 10cm (4in)
of footside. Plot two points diagonally from each of these,
points *4-9* etc. (figure 72). The diamond of points *10-13* is

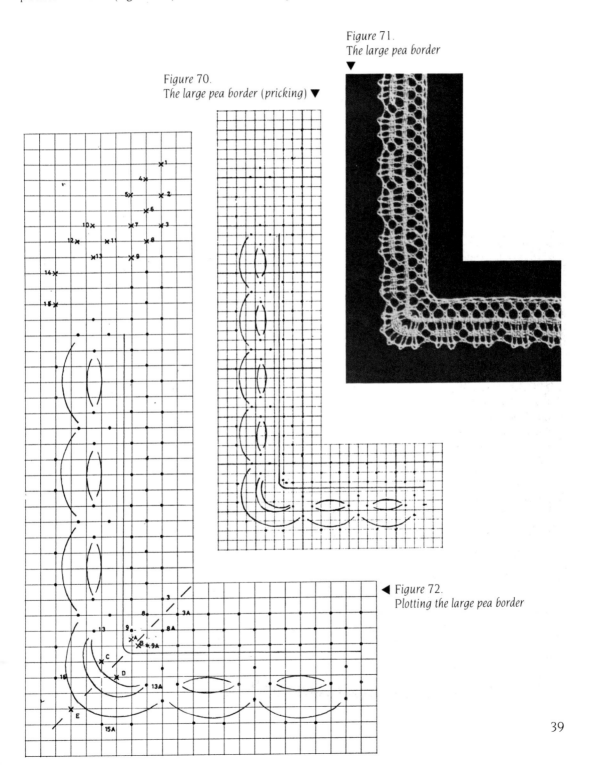

Figure 71.
The large pea border
▼

Figure 70.
The large pea border (pricking) ▼

◄ Figure 72.
Plotting the large pea border

displaced half a square to the left allowing extra space for the passives. Point *10* is placed two and a half squares to the left of point *7*, point *11* two and a half squares to the left of, point *8*, point *12* two squares to the left of point *11* and point *13* two and a half squares to the left of point *9*. Point *14* is placed on the horizontal line below point *13*, on the seventh vertical line from the footside. Point *15* lies on the second line below point *14*. Repeat for the length of the footside. Draw the guidelines.

For the corner, plot as far as points *3, 8, 9, 13* and *15* and mark the points diagonally across the squares from points *3, 8* and *9* at *3A, 8A* and *9A*. From point *3A* continue the footside for the new section at right angles to the original section. Plot the two lines of ground, the diamond and headside points for the new section. Place points *A* and *B* near points *9* and *9A*, as shown, then points *C, D* and *E*. Draw the guidelines.

GERMAN SPIDER (figures 73 and 74)
This is a firm border that launders well. Start by plotting points *1* and *2* and continue for about 10cm (4in) of footside. Mark two rows of ground next to the footside starting from points *3* and *4* and *5* and *6* (figure 75). Mark point *7* to the left of point *5*, point *8* on the third line to the left of point *7* and point *9* on the second line to the left of point *8*. Point *10* is situated on the line to the left of point *9* and two squares below it. Points *11* and *12* are evenly spaced in the gaps between the points *8*.

For the corner, plot as far as points *2, 4, 5, 7, 9* and *12*. Mark points *2A, 4A* and *5A* diagonally across the squares from points *2, 4* and *5*. Plot the new section of footside, at right angles to the original section, starting from point *2A*. Plot the two rows of ground starting from points *4A* and *5A* respectively and the remaining points for the new section. Mark points *A* and *B* on the intersections near points *7* and *7A*, points *C* and *D* on the intersections between points *12* and *12A* and points *E* and *F* between points *9* and *9A*. Draw the guidelines.

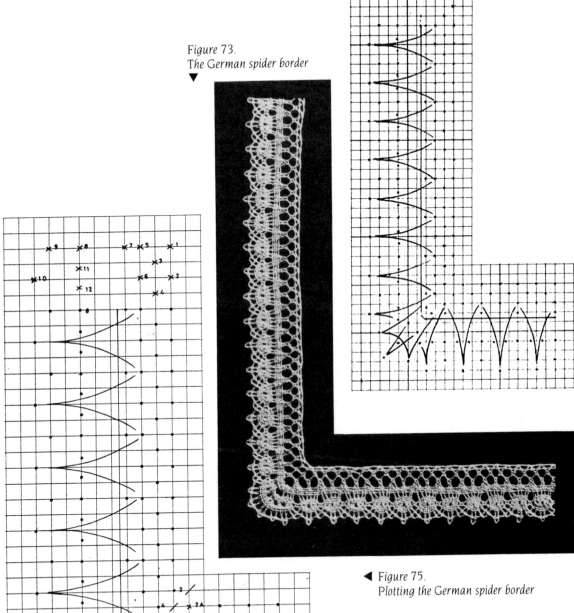

Figure 73.
The German spider border
▼

Figure 74.
The German spider border (pricking)
▼

◀ Figure 75.
Plotting the German spider border

41

Figure 77.
The scallop border (pricking)

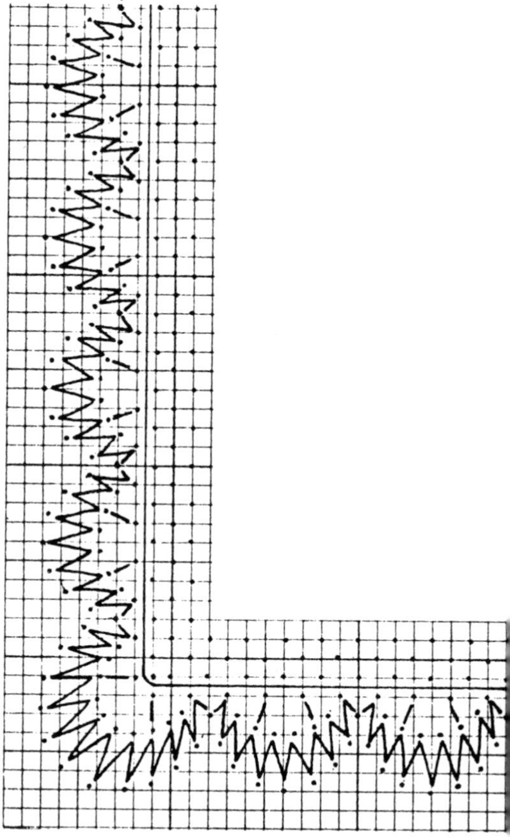

Figure 76.
The scallop border

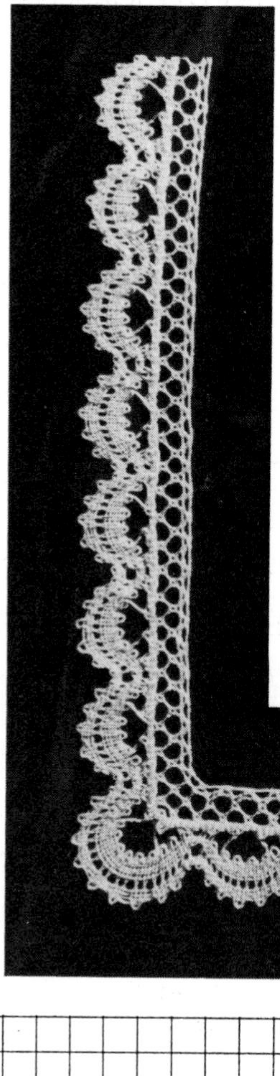

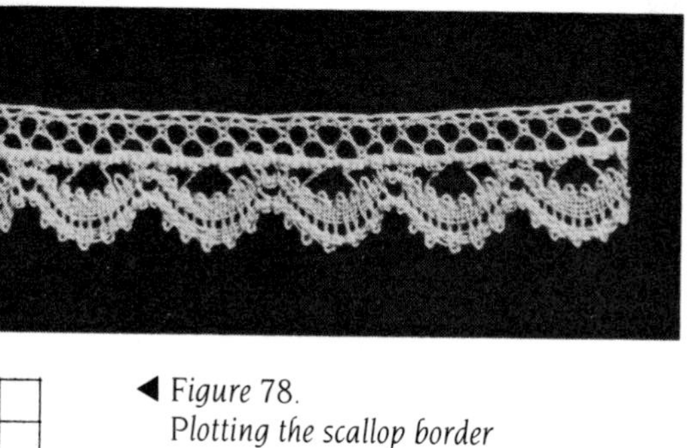

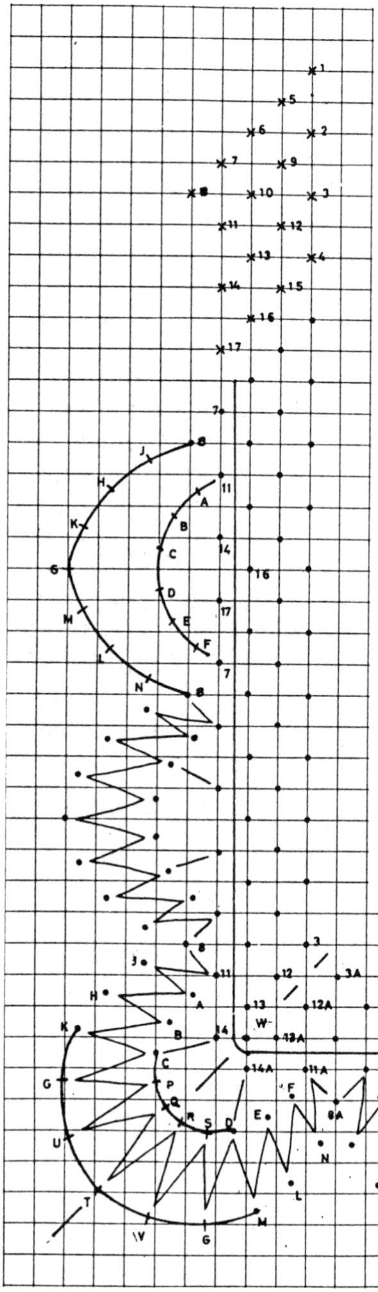

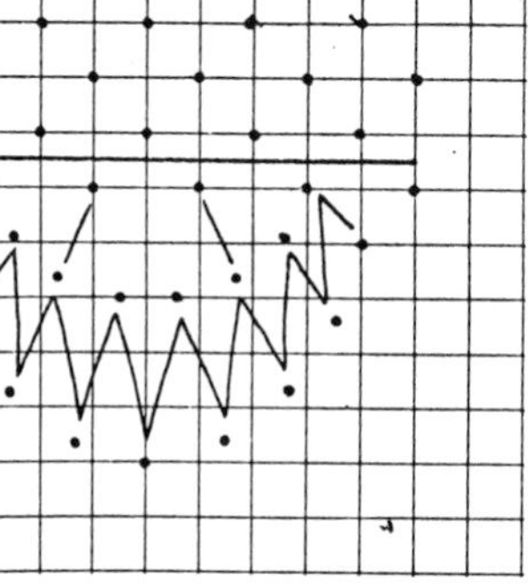

Figure 78.
Plotting the scallop border

SCALLOP (figures 76 and 77)

If required, this border can be drawn allowing extra room for the passives. From points *1-4* plot about 10cm (4in) of footside and mark points *5-17* diagonally from these for the length of the footside (figure 78). Draw the inner curve of the scallop between points *11* and *7* extending as far as the second line to the left of these points. Place six points *A-F*, equally spaced, along this curve. Draw the outer curve between points *8* extending as far as the fourth line to the left of these points. This curve has been drawn with a slight 'peak' in the centre. To achieve this, plot point *G* on the sixth vertical line to the left of point *16*. The curve through points *8, J, H, K* and *G* is drawn as part of a circle with its centre at point *17* and the curve through points *G, M, L, N* and *8* is drawn as part of a circle with its centre at point *14*. Six points *H, J-M* and *N* are placed, evenly spaced, along the curve. These points are plotted in the easiest order, namely the centre point, the mid-point of each half and then the mid-point of each section. Draw the guideline.

The 'peaked' scallop can be successfully worked because a pair of passives is brought from the band of passives at pin *14*, included as a passive in the scallop from pins *B-E* and returned to the band of plain passives at pin *17*.

For the corner, plot as far as points *3, 8* and *11-14* and mark points *3A* and *12A-14A* diagonally across the corner squares from points *3* and *12-14*. From the footside point *3A* plot the new section of footside at right angles to the original section. Using a transparent template for the curves prick points *A, B, C, J, H, K* and *G* for the section of the corner adjacent to the original section and points *D, E, F, G, M, L* and *N* for the section of the corner adjacent to the new section. Draw the remaining portions of the curves for the corner and mark four points *P-S* between points *C* and *D* of the inner curve and three points *T-V* between the two points *G* of the outer curve. The points *G* may be 'moved' to even the spacing if necessary. Draw the guidelines.

DECORATED FANS AND BORDERS

Fringes are not usually considered as part of traditional torchon lace and the plaited decoration is probably more Cluny than traditional torchon. However, they have been included for those who wish to embellish their lace. After all, lace is designed to please the maker, not to fit in with a rigid set of rules.

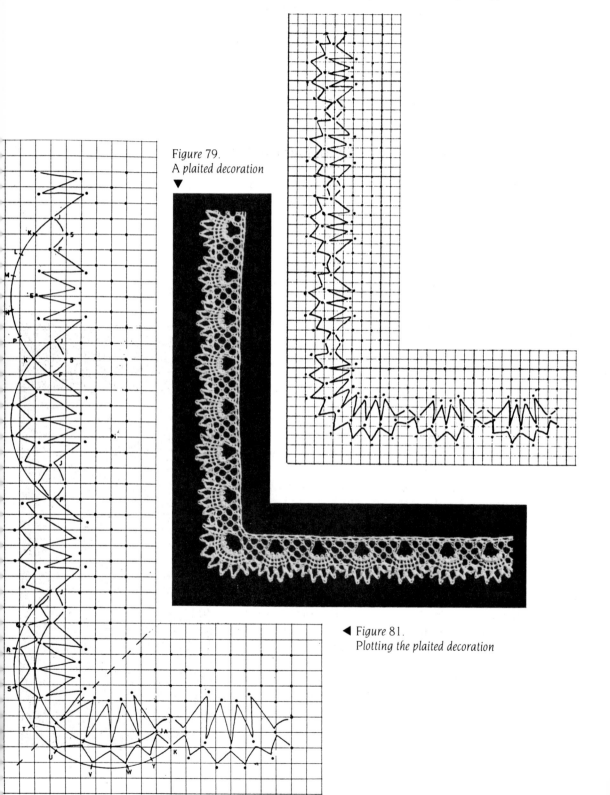

Figure 80.
A *plaited decoration* (pricking)

Figure 79.
A *plaited decoration*
▼

◀ Figure 81.
Plotting the plaited decoration

PLAITED DECORATION (figures 79 and 80)

This decoration may be used in conjunction with many fan and border patterns. The fan or border pattern is generally plotted in the usual way, a line is then drawn following the headside at a distance of one to two squares from it. The points for the peaks of the plaits are placed approximately mid-way between the headside points of the fan or border pattern; their final positions being modified by the positions of the adjacent plaits. Sometimes the plaits are curved using two or more pins to hold them in shape; sometimes they are decorated by one or more picots. This particular design is based on the scallop or coronet fan. Plot the fan as previously described (figure 81). Draw the curve for the points of the plaits between points *J* and *F* extending one and a half squares beyond point *E*. If these curves are drawn for adjacent fans they will be seen to cross at point *K*. Mark points *L, M, N* and *P* on the curve so they are situated mid-way between the points *K-K* along the outer curve of the original fan. Since these points are somewhat unevenly distributed they can be 'moved' slightly to make a more even arrangement, bearing in mind that the positions of the peaks of the plaits relative to the points along the fan are also important. The corner is marked similarly.

FRINGE (figures 82 and 83)

A fringe can be worked along most of the fans and borders. In this case it has been worked in conjunction with the Spanish fan. A contrasting thickness or colour of thread may be used for the worker of the fan and fringe if required. Draw the Spanish fan as previously described. Select a vertical line to the left of the fans so that the distance between the fans and this line is a little longer than the required length of the fringe (figure 84). Draw horizontal lines connecting this line and points *2-7* along the curves of the fans, marking the points *2A-7A* where they meet along the selected vertical line. Make the lace, as far as pin *2*. Take the workers round pin *2A* and return to pin *2*. Remove and replace the pin under the workers. Repeat for pins *3-7* and *3A-7A*. Alternatively, prick holes *2-7* sufficiently large so as to take two pins. After setting up pin *2* taking the workers round pin *2A* and, returning to pin *2*, set up another pin under the workers in the hole. This method may seem clumsy but it produces good results. If possible leave the work to set for a week.

Finally clip the ends of the loops of the fringe along the cutting line and remove the pins. Trim the fringe if required.

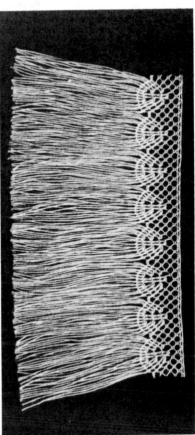

Figure 82.
A *fringed border*

Figure 83.
A fringed border (pricking)

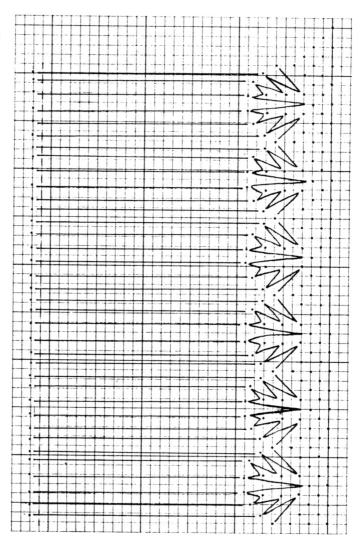

Figure 84
Plotting the fringed border
▼

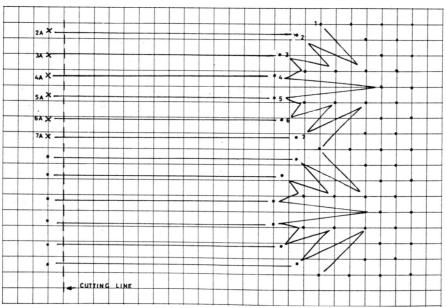

CUTTING LINE

7.
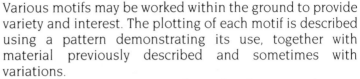
Motifs within the Ground and Copying Patterns

Various motifs may be worked within the ground to provide variety and interest. The plotting of each motif is described using a pattern demonstrating its use, together with material previously described and sometimes with variations.

Practise copying patterns from the diagrams, then try copying from prickings using similar sequences. Also compare the copying sequence with a photograph of the lace. A transparent ruler laid along the lines of the pin positions in the lace makes counting easier.

Figure 85.
Diamonds in the ground

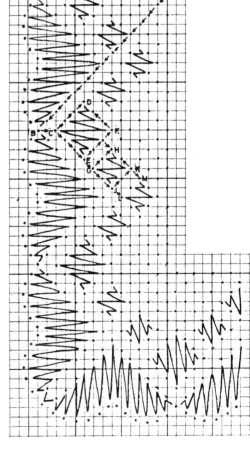

Figure 86.
Diamonds in the ground (pricking)▶

47

DIAMONDS (figures 85 and 86)

When diamonds of whole or half stitch are to be included in the lace an open space is left within the ground, the points bordering the space being used to work the motif. To copy this pattern plot a line of footside points, then count and plot the longest row of points A-B across the pattern. This establishes the position of the low point B between the hearts. Count then plot the number of points along each 'leg' of the zig-zag boundary of the hearts for at least three pattern repeats. The large diamond is placed within the point of the zig-zag. Count the number of points along each side of the diamond then, plotting as for torchon ground, mark points C-D, C-E and D-F-E. The guideline helps to illustrate the effect of the diamond in the pattern. The points bounding the space belong to the diamond and cannot be used as the border for any other motif. Count the number of points along each side of a small diamond. Plot the rows of points G-H adjacent to the large diamond and points G-J adjacent to the border of the heart. Complete the remaining sides, points H-K-J. Now plot the side of the next diamond, points L-M and its remaining sides. Pass on to the next large diamond, then the smaller one between. Plot the torchon ground between the diamonds and the footside. Draw the heart-shaped fans as previously described, checking that the correct number of points has been plotted along the curve when the guideline is drawn. Diamonds cannot straddle a corner although they can be used immediately next to it.

TRIANGLES (figures 87 and 88)

These open spaces within the ground extend to the footside. The sides bordering the ground are plotted as usual but the footside requires special treatment, usually having one less point than the other two sides combined.

Here the footside does not follow its usual pattern; starting at point A, count and plot the number of points along the other two sides of the triangle, i.e. points A-B-C. Count and plot the number of points between A and C along the footside. Most of these are located half-way between pairs of lines but those near points A or C may need 'moving' to make the spacing more even. Draw the guideline. To compensate for the closeness of the pins, reduce the number of twists when working the footside. The points for rose ground are plotted as for torchon ground. From point B plot points D and E and mark two rows of points, as for torchon ground, following the zig-zag points of the triangle. Draw the 'diamond' guidelines characteristic of rose ground.

From point E find the position of point F on the inner boundary of the fan. This is not a low point between fans but

Figure 87
Triangles at the footside

Figure 88.
Triangles at the footside (pricking)

half-way along one side, so count and plot points *F-G*, then to point *H*. The zig-zag boundary of the fans can now be marked, then the fans plotted as previously described.

Triangles at the footside variation (figures 89 and 90)
An attractive variation uses another line of pins just inside an ordinary footside.

Plot the footside then count and plot the longest line of points *A-B* across the pattern establishing the position of the low point between the fans. Count then plot the points of the zig-zag boundary of the fans. Mark a line of points on alternate lines next to the footside starting from point *C*. Count then plot the points *C-D-E*, the zig-zag boundary of the triangles, noting where the two zig-zag boundaries meet and the triangle boundary meets the line of points next to the footside. Plot the rose ground squares between the two boundaries as for torchon ground and draw the guidelines.

This Spanish fan has been reduced in depth from point to curve and does not have the usual extra point beyond the zig-zag boundary at the low point between the fans. This means that the points of the central division must be adjusted accordingly.

Figure 89.
Triangle at the footside, variation ▶

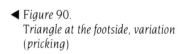

◀ *Figure 90.*
Triangle at the footside, variation (pricking)

Triangles pointing up or down (figures 91 and 92)
When the lace is worked the triangles always appear smaller than the space allotted to them. Plot the footside, then count and plot a long line of points *A-B* diagonally across the pattern, excluding the plain border, to establish its width. From point *A* count as far as point *C*, the apex of the triangle. Starting from point *C* count and plot down the other side of the triangle to point *D*. Mark the guideline for the triangle. Plot three lines of torchon ground below the triangle. The first between points *B* and *D*, then the rows of points *E-F*, and *G-H*. Count and plot the sides of the next triangle, points *G-J* and *H-J*. Draw the guideline for this triangle. Plot the diagonal line of points between the next

Figure 91.
Triangles pointing up and down ▶

Figure 92.
Triangles pointing up and down
(pricking)
▼

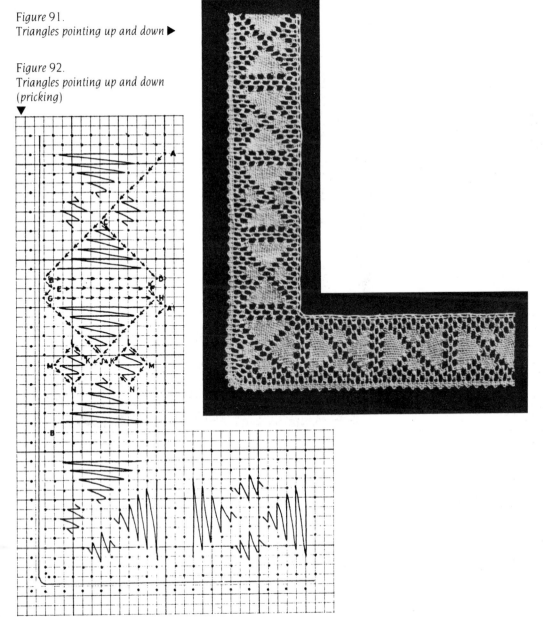

points A and B. Plot the points K-L-M-N returning to K for the diamonds. Plot torchon ground between the triangles, diamonds and the footside, and between the triangles, diamonds and the vertical line through point B, including the points along this line. Plot the headside points for the plain border as previously described. Triangles of whole or half stitch cannot be worked straddling a corner. This lace sample was worked using whole stitch for the diamonds and triangles and a whole stitch and twist torchon ground.

Figure 93.
Hearts in the ground

Figure 94.
Hearts in the ground (pricking)

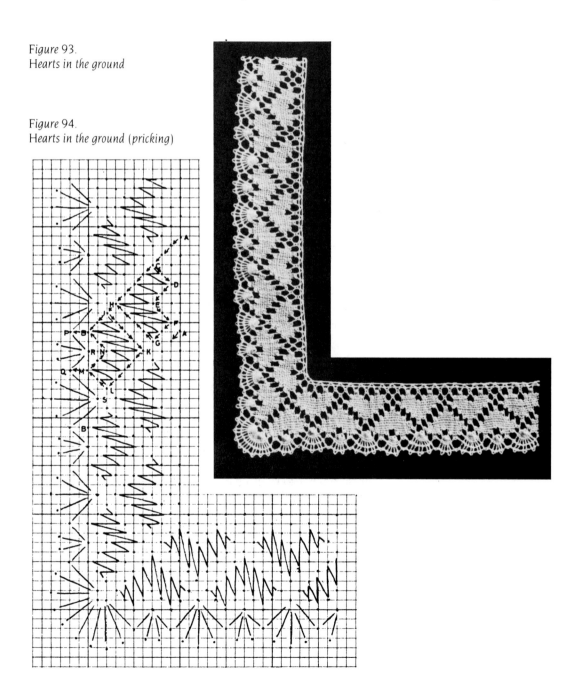

HEARTS (figures 93 and 94)

Hearts within a pattern are very angular, their sides following the pattern of points as for torchon ground.

Start copying this pattern by plotting the footside, then counting and plotting the longest row of points *A-B* across the pattern. Then count and plot the points of the heart closest to the footside. Establish the topmost point of the heart, point *C* by counting from point *A*. Then count and plot from point *C* to points *D-E-F-G* and to point *H*. Check by counting points *C-H*. Draw the guideline. From point *J* next to point *H*, count and plot around the next heart, points *J-K-L-M-N* and to point *B*. Check the number of points *B-J*. Draw the guide line. Plot the next line of points *A-B*. Continue plotting the hearts, then the torchon ground between these and the footside. In this pattern the edges of the hearts form the inner border for the French fans, and points *P* and *Q* are required two lines to the left of the peaks of the zig-zag. Draw the curves for these fans as previously described and plot the points along them. Plot point *R* between points *B* and *M* and point *S* next to point *L*. Note that two sizes of fan have been used with different numbers of points along the headsides. Since both fans are small, only one point is necessary for the worker to 'wrap around'.

TRAILS (figures 95 and 96)

Narrow trails can be worked between adjacent rows of torchon ground whereas wider trails usually have one, or occasionally more, rows of points omitted from the ground. Since trails are continuous it is difficult to count the number of points across the pattern or lace and the width of the trail must be estimated. For this pattern estimate the number of points to be omitted by placing a ruler, preferably transparent, along the rows of holes in the pattern or the corresponding positions in the lace. Place the ruler along either side of the trail and note how many rows of holes lie between these positions. These can be seen best beyond the trails. Check by testing another portion of the trail.

For this pattern place the ruler along the rows of points *A-B*, *C-D* and *E-F*. When the ruler lies along row *E-F* five points have been omitted where it passes through the centre of the trail. Check by placing the ruler along the rows of points *G-H*, *J-K* and *L-M* where a similar omission has occurred along the row *L-M*. Thus, for this pattern, a single line of points has been omitted through the centre of the trail for its entire length. Mark a section of footside then count and plot the number of points *C-N*. This establishes the position of the trail closest to the footside. Count and plot the points of this side of the trail along the footside and mark the torchon ground between them. From point *N* count and plot across the trail to point *P*, the other side of the trail, i.e. omitting one point as previously estimated. Plot the points for the other side of the trail by counting the numbers of points along each section of the zig-zag. Draw the guideline for the trail. In this pattern two trails meet at regular intervals. Starting from one of these points *Q* count and plot to point *R* and to the next point *Q*. Continue marking this side of the second trail for the length of the pattern. Plot the torchon ground between the trails. From

Figure 95.
Trails in the ground ▶

Figure 96.
Trails in the ground (pricking)

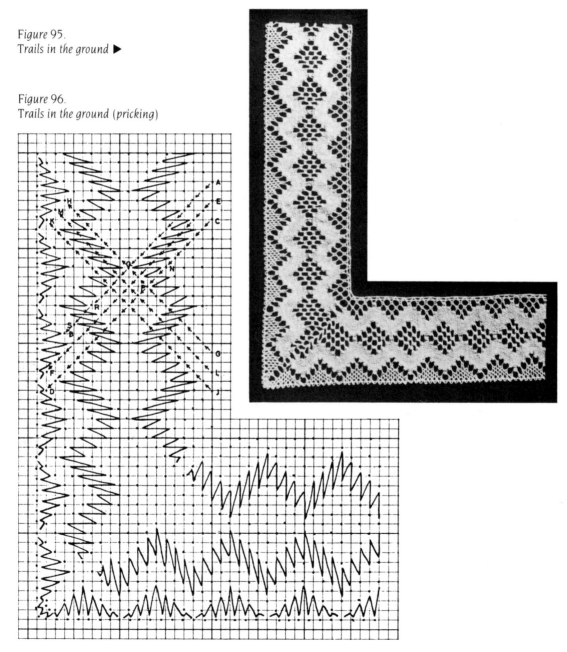

point *R* find the position of point *S*, the other side of the trail, and continue plotting the remainder of the trail. Draw the guideline. Plot the zig-zag row of points for the fans and complete them as previously described.

Except for very narrow trails worked in half stitch, trails cannot be worked across the diagonal through the corner and must be terminated and restarted adjacent to this diagonal. The ends of the trail on either side of the break are worked as the end or beginning of a diamond.

Figure 97.
Spiders in the ground ▶

Figure 98.
Spiders in the ground (pricking)

SPIDERS (figures 97 and 98)

Spiders are worked within diamond-shaped spaces in torchon ground. A central point is required for working the spider. The points along the edge of the spider may be shared with the next motif.

To copy this pattern count, then plot the points A-B, the longest row possible. Then count and plot the zig-zag of points forming the inner border of the trail edge. Count and plot around the diamond shapes for the spiders and place a single point in the centre of each space. Draw the guidelines for the spiders. Mark the torchon ground between the spiders and the footside. Next, estimate the width of the trail edge. By placing a ruler along the rows between points C and D and E and F the two rows can be seen to cross at point G. The position of point H is more difficult to estimate. If copying from a pricking or lace it is best estimated by measuring the distance between points B and H and comparing it with the distance between points of the ground. This does not always give an accurate result but fans are flexible and if in doubt check the pricking by working a small portion before embarking on a large project.

TALLIES (figures 99 and 101)

Some tallies are worked within the structure of the torchon ground. To copy the pattern plot a row of points for the footside, and count then plot a long line of torchon ground, points A-B, omitting a point at C, as described previously for the pea border. Plot the headside row of points from point B. Count from point A to D, then count and plot the points forming the diamond space containing the four spiders, points D-E-F-G. Plot point H two lines below point F and mark a similar diamond for the single spider. Continue plotting diamonds for the length required. Plot torchon ground between the footside and the headside avoiding the diamond spaces and the intersection at C as described previously for the pea border. Note that this pattern is a variation on the pea border and has the point at J, adjacent to C omitted. Draw the guidelines for the pea border and the half stitch trails. Since the trails are narrow, and in half stitch, they do not need to be broken as they cross the corner. The tallies are worked diagonally within the diamonds of the torchon ground and are indicated by large spots. Plot the centres of the single spiders within the diamonds, then the sets of four spiders. One way of finding the positions of these spider 'centres' is to imagine, or lightly sketch, the diamond that the spider would occupy if it were a single one (figure 100). In this case the diamond for the upper spider would be bounded by points J, K, L and M. The centre is easy to find at point N. The diamond for the left spider is bounded by points *P, Q, R* and *S* with its centre at point *T*. Use the same method for finding the 'centres' of the other two spiders.

Another method is to draw the 'V' shapes for the legs of the spiders along the boundary (figure 102). Lightly sketch the lines across the diamond through these 'V's. The centres of the spiders occur at the intersections of these lines, i.e. the line between legs *U* and *V* intersects the one between legs *W* and *Y* at point *Z*.

Figure 99.
Tallies in the ground (pricking)

Figure 100.
Finding the centres for compound spiders by sketching their squares

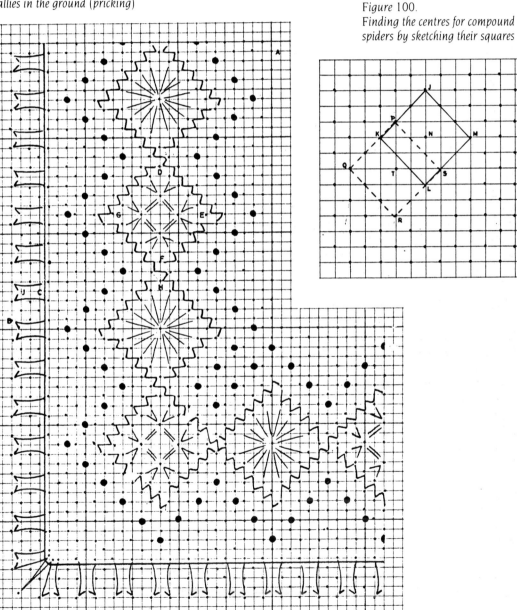

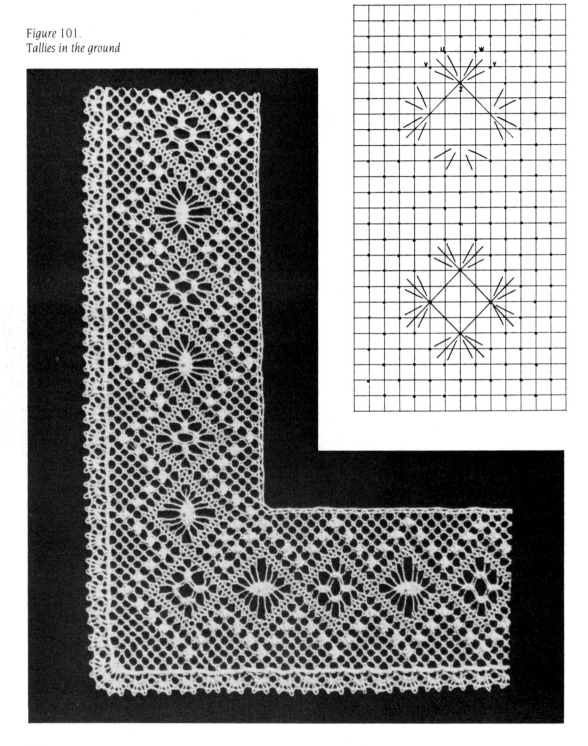

Figure 101.
Tallies in the ground

Figure 102.
Finding the centres for compound
spiders from the positions of their legs

58

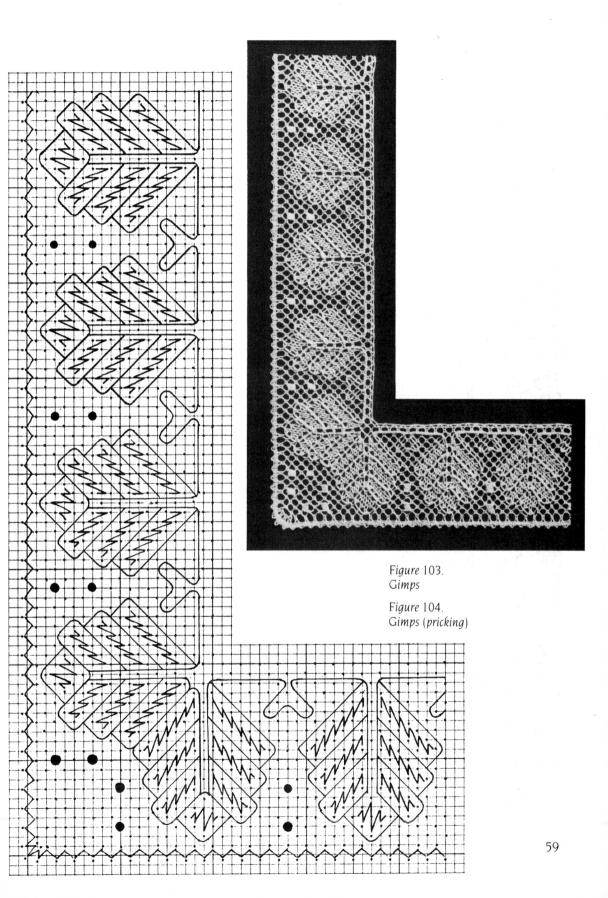

Figure 103.
Gimps

Figure 104.
Gimps (pricking)

59

GIMPS (figures 103 and 104)

Lines are drawn between the motifs and points of the ground to indicate the position of the gimps. To copy this pattern plot a line of footside points and count and plot a diagonal row of points to establish the width of the pattern excluding the plain border. Plot an area of torchon ground this width from the footside and plot the plain edge as previously described. Draw the guidelines for the half stitch strips after carefully counting each section. Draw the gimp around the section before passing on to the next. The torchon ground point within the half stitch diamond is omitted. The tallies in this pattern are worked straight and the spots that indicate their presence replace points of the torchon ground.

FILLINGS (figures 105 and 106)

Many fancy filling stitches are used to decorate torchon lace. Before introducing a filling into a pattern familiarize yourself with its structure by plotting a small portion and check that it will fit into its allotted space. Sometimes patterns are modified to provide the required space. The best corners are those with sections of filling meeting at the corner, or the corner passing through the filling with one half completed before, and the remainder after, turning the corner. However sometimes the position of the corner is not in an ideal position for the filling. In this situation rows of torchon ground may be introduced between the line through the corner and the areas of the filling.

   Using a ruler to examine the positions of the pinholes around the trails it can be seen that they are narrow, i.e. the distance between two rows of torchon ground points. Start copying the pattern by plotting a row of points for the footside. Count then plot the row of points *A-B* to establish the position of the headside trail. Count then plot the row of points *C-D* to establish point *D* one corner of the space containing the filling. Continue counting and plotting the rows of points *E-F-G*, the boundary of the filling. From point *C* count to point *H* then count and plot rows of points *H-L-K-J* around the space for the spider, and then the points around the other spider. Starting from point *B* count and plot the inner border of the headside trail noting that the number of points varies for alternate peaks. Draw the curved edge of the headside, allowing more room for the extra passive pairs between the curve and the smaller peak than between the curve and the larger peak. Plot torchon ground between the footside and the inner border of the headside trail, omitting the areas for the fancy filling and the spiders. Draw the guidelines for the trails and the spiders. Finally plot the filling and draw its guidelines.

60

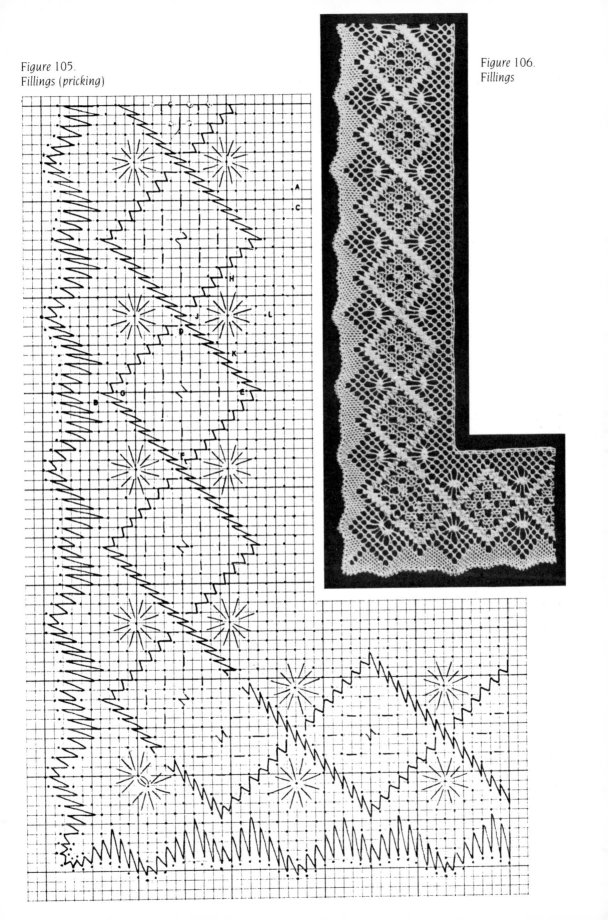

Figure 105.
Fillings (pricking)

Figure 106.
Fillings

8.
Changing Scale

One advantage of being able to draft patterns is the ability to draw them to a suitable scale. Lace intended for household use will require a coarser thread and a pattern drawn to a larger scale than one for a handkerchief edging. It is interesting to see how the aesthetic effect varies as the scale becomes smaller, the individual stitches become less important and the overall impression created by the different areas changes.

DIFFERENT SCALES OF GRAPH PAPER

The most useful sizes of graph paper currently available are ¹/₁₀in (2.5mm) and 2mm. So far all the patterns have been drawn on ¹/₁₀in (2.5mm) graph paper requiring a 50 linen or thread of similar thickness for the lace (figures 107 and 108). If the same sequences of points are plotted on 2mm paper the spacing between the pins will be approximately ⅘ that of the pattern on ¹/₁₀in paper and will require an 80 or 90 linen thread for the lace (figures 107 and 109).

PLOTTING DIAGONALLY ACROSS THE PAPER

By drawing the patterns diagonally across the same graph papers, prickings suitable for finer threads will be produced. Patterns drawn diagonally across ¹/₁₀in (2.5mm) graph paper will produce a pattern requiring DMC Retors d'Alsace No. 30 (figures 107 and 110) and patterns drawn diagonally across 2mm graph paper can be worked using DMC Retors d'Alsace No. 50 (figures 107 and 111).

When the pattern is plotted diagonally the footside points are plotted on every intersection. Lines of points extending diagonally across the finished pattern are plotted on every intersection along lines of the graph paper. Torchon ground is plotted using all the intersections. Compare the versions of the pattern on the different graph papers. Note that the 'centres' of the spiders are sometimes placed in the centres of graph paper squares.

Figure 107.
(Top) *Lace made on a pattern drawn on ¹/₁₀in (2.5mm) graph paper straight. Lace worked in Bockens No. 50 linen.*
(Upper middle) *Lace made on a pattern drawn on 2mm graph paper straight. Lace worked in Bockens No. 80 linen*
(Lower middle) *Lace made on a pattern drawn on ¹/₁₀in (2.5mm) graph paper diagonally. lace worked in DMC Retors d'Alsace No. 30 cotton*
(Bottom) *Lace made on a pattern drawn on 2mm graph paper diagonally. Lace worked in DMC Retors d'Alsace No. 50 cotton*

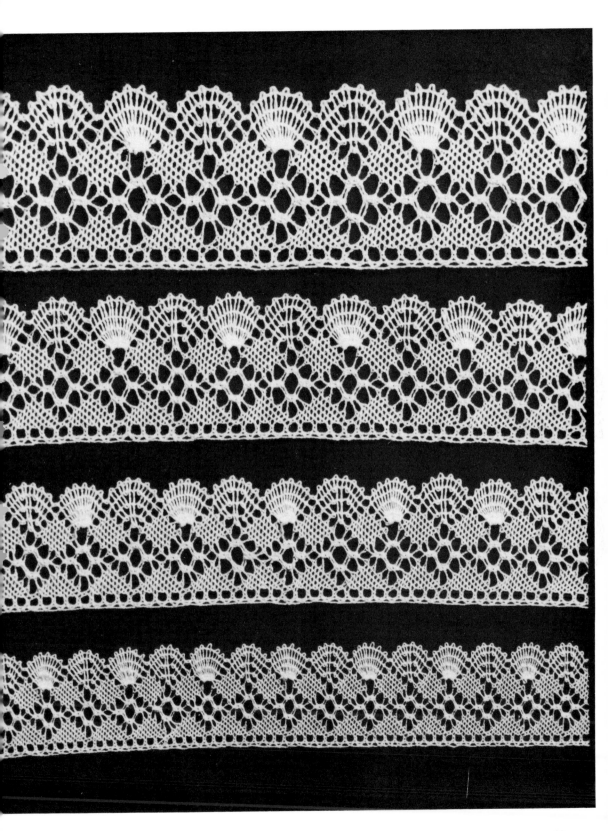

63

THREAD CHART

The following chart was worked out using the same pattern drawn straight or diagonally on various graph papers.

The distances between the pins have been calculated and included for anyone interested although I have not found them particularly helpful myself. What *has* proved useful is knowing the number of pins per 10cm (4in) measured along the footside. When selecting a thread for a torchon pricking, measure that distance along the footside and count the holes; it is then easy to select a suitable thread from the chart.

Another use of the chart is the comparison of threads. The threads are listed according to thickness and the way the thread is worked up. If a pattern suggests a thread you do

Figure 108.
Pattern drawn on ¹/₁₀in (2.5mm) graph paper (straight)

Figure 109.
Pattern drawn on 2mm graph paper (straight)

Figure 110.
Pattern drawn on ¹/₁₀in (2.5mm) graph paper (diagonally)

not possess, it may be possible to substitute the next one one the chart or, in fact, any of those in the same group. However, it is necessary to bear in mind that all threads vary slightly in size and body and will work up closer, stiffer or softer according to the material from which it is made and the quality of the finish.

This chart is not intended to dictate rigidly the threads that should be used. I have selected pattern sizes for the threads that result in a medium weight lace, but for handkerchief edgings and other lace that will need to withstand hard wear and washing a thicker thread than those recommended may be more suitable, whereas a finer thread may be required for lace that is to be mounted under glass. Try using up those odd ends left on bobbins at the completion of a piece of lace to make a small sample on a pattern of a different size. You may prefer the result. Using different threads and different pattern sizes is the only way to acquire the experience needed to be able to match thread and pattern to produce the result you desire.

Figure 111
Pattern drawn on 2mm graph paper
(diagonally)

5mm graph paper (diagonal)

Distance between pins measured on the straight of the ground	7.1mm
Distance between pins measured diagonally across the ground	5.0mm
Number of pins per 10cm (4in) measured along the footside	14

Threads 20/2 C & F linen (B.O.U.C.) natural
           16/2 Bockens linen
           5 D.M.C. Perle

⅛in graph paper (straight)

Distance between pins measured on the straight of the ground	6.3mm
Distance between pins measured diagonally across the ground	4.5mm
Number of pins per 10cm (4in) measured along the footside	15

Threads 8 D.M.C. Perle
           50/2 C & F linen (B.O.U.C.) natural

1/10in graph paper (*straight*)

Distance between pins measured on the straight of the ground	5.1mm
Distance between pins measured diagonally across the ground	3.6mm
Number of pins per 10cm (4in) measured along the footside	19

Threads   35 Bockens linen
50/2 C & F linen (B.O.U.C.) white
25 D.M.C. Coton à Broder
60 D.M.C. Cordonnet Special
50 Bockens linen
60 Bockens linen
   D.M.C. Fil à Dentelles

1/8in graph paper (*diagonal*)

Distance between pins measured on the straight of the ground	4.5mm
Distance between pins measured diagonally across the ground	3.2mm
Number of pins per 10cm (4in) measured along the footside	22

Threads   60 Bockens linen
   D.M.C. Fil à Dentelles

1/12in graph paper (*straight*)

Distance between pins measured on the straight of the ground	4.2mm
Distance between pins measured diagonally across the ground	3.0mm
Number of pins per 10cm (4in) measured along the footside	23

Threads   D.M.C. Fil à Dentelles
   80 Bockens linen

2mm graph paper (*straight*)

Distance between pins measured on the straight of the ground	4mm
Distance between pins measured diagonally across the ground	2.8mm
Number of pins per 10cm (4in) measured along the footside	25

Threads   80/3 spun silk (Piper)
            80 D.M.C. Cordonnet Special
            80 Bockens linen

1/10in graph paper (diagonal)

Distance between pins measured on the
    straight of the ground   3.6mm
Distance between pins measured diagonally
    across the ground   2.5mm
Number of pins per 10cm (4in) measured
    along the footside   27

Threads   30 D.M.C. Brilliante d'Alsace
            80/2 C & F linen (B.O.U.C.) white
            100 D.M.C. Cordonnet Special
            30 D.M.C. Retors d'Alsace
            90 Bockens linen
            100/2 C & F linen (B.O.U.C.) white
            120/2 C & F linen (B.O.U.C.) natural

1/16in graph paper (straight)

Distance between pins measured on the
    straight of the ground   3.2mm
Distance between pins measured diagonally
    across the ground   2.3mm
Number of pins per 10cm (4in) measured
    along the footside   31

Threads   120/2 C & F linen (B.O.U.C.) white
            30 D.M.C. Retors d'Alsace

1/12in graph paper (diagonal)

Distance between pins measured on the
    straight of the ground   3.0mm
Distance between pins measured diagonally
    across the ground   2.1mm
Number of pins per 10cm (4in) measured
    along the footside   33

Threads   140/2 C & F linen (B.O.U.C.) (when available)
            80 English Sewing Ltd. Unity

2mm graph paper (*diagonal*)
Distance between pins measured on the
   straight of the ground   2.8mm
Distance between pins measured diagonally
   across the ground   2.0mm
Number of pins per 10cm (4in) measured
   along the footside   35

Threads   50 D.M.C. Retors d'Alsace
          90-100 denir silk (Piper)
          50 D.M.C. Brilliante d'Alsace
          100 English Sewing Ltd. Unity

$1/20$in *graph paper* (*straight*)
Distance between pins measured on the
   straight of the ground   2.6mm
Distance between pins measured diagonally
   across the ground   1.8mm
Number of pins per 10cm (4in) measured
   along the footside   39

Threads   50 D.M.C. Retors d'Alsace
          100 English Sewing Ltd. Unity

1mm graph paper (*straight*)
Distance between pins measured on the
   straight of the ground   2.0mm
Distance between pins measured diagonally
   across the ground   1.4mm
Number of pins per 10cm (4in) measured
   along the footside   49

Threads   80 Brok
          100 Brok
          80 Honiton thread
          100 Honiton thread

$1/20$in *graph paper* (*diagonal*)
Distance between pins measured on the
   straight of the ground   1.8mm
Distance between pins measured diagonally
   across the ground   1.3mm
Number of pins per 10cm (4in) measured
   along the footside   54

Threads   100 Brok
            100 Honiton thread
            120 Honiton thread

1mm graph paper (diagonal)
Distance between pins measured on the
    straight of the ground   1.4mm
Distance between pins measured diagonally
    across the ground   1.0mm
Number of pins per 10cm (4in) measured
    along the footside   70

Threads   120 Honiton thread
            160 Honiton thread

9.
Adapting Patterns

An edging may be adapted to form a corner, provide a fancy corner for a handkerchief, be turned into an insertion to accompany an edging, or converted into a bookmark, mat, paperweight or brooch motif. Possible adaptations can be clearly seen by placing a plain rectangular mirror on the pattern or lace in certain positions.

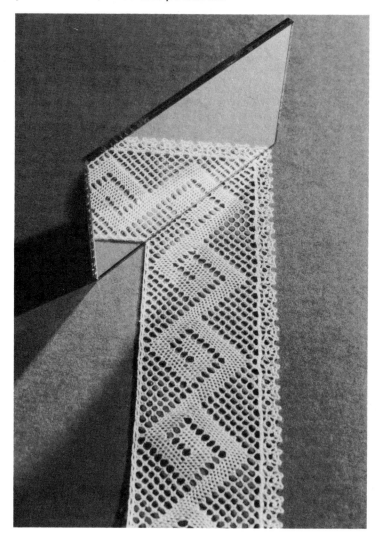

Figure 112
Using a mirror to design a corner.
Greek key pattern from the
collections of Mrs Vi Bullard and
Mrs Joan Savage.

CORNERS (figures 112-114)
When designing a corner for an edging try standing a mirror
vertically on the lace or pattern at 45 degrees to the footside
(figures 112, 113 and 114). Slide the mirror along the lace,
maintaining this angle to the footside, note any 'corners'
that look as though they might work and try plotting them.

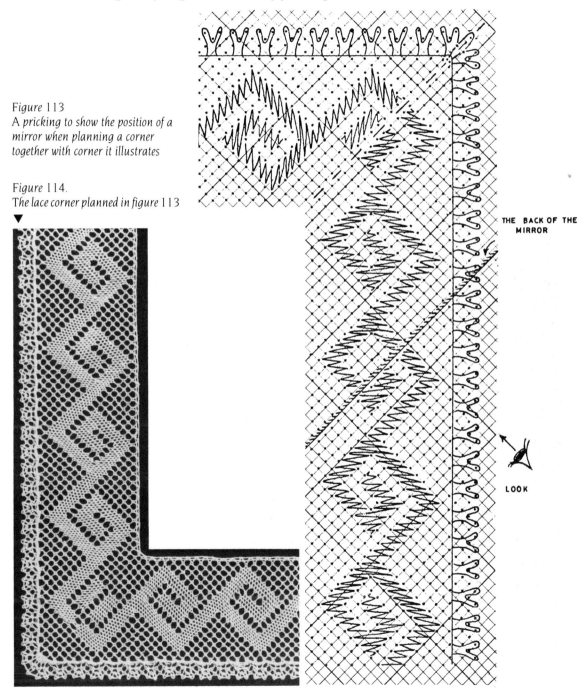

Figure 113
A *pricking to show the position of a
mirror when planning a corner
together with corner it illustrates*

Figure 114.
The lace corner planned in figure 113

THE BACK OF THE
MIRROR

LOOK

Some patterns have only one possible corner, others several. Bear in mind the following limitations.

(a) Torchon corners rarely have a line of pins through the corner since it causes problems when making the lace, a new pair having to be introduced at one end of this line and removed at the other. Instead the actual corner is usually situated midway between two rows of points.

(b) The plain fan cannot be worked around a corner, instead, one fan must be completed immediately before and the next one immediately after the corner.

(c) The fir tree, scallop and Paris fans usually have the centre point of the inner boundary 'V' of the fan placed immediately before and a similar point placed immediately after the corner. The fan is adapted and worked around the corner. The corner for the feather fan, already described, is a modification of this.

(d) Spiders cannot be placed centrally across the corner although spiders placed adjacent to it may have their 'shared legs' lying across it.

(e) Most trails within the lace must be 'broken' when they cross the corner with extra points inserted at their ends if they are wide. The narrow half-stitch trail is an exception. Other half-stitch trails can be made to cross the corner if back stitches are strategically used.

(f) Whole and half-stitch motifs cannot straddle the corner. Sometimes a 'half or part motif' is completed immediately before, and another 'half or part motif' worked immediately after the corner.

(g) Since fillings consist of sets of stitches, worked using a set number of pins, there are only certain positions for the corner where the filling can be worked using the pins on either side of the line through the corner. If, due to the characteristics of other features in the pattern, the corner cannot be placed in an ideal position for the filling, then rows of torchon ground may be introduced adjacent to the line through the corner.

As the corners previously described illustrate these points, try standing a mirror on a straight section of the patterns and look for any other corners that could have been used.

SIDE REVERSE (figures 115 and 116)
Torchon patterns are usually the same when inverted. However, sometimes this method of designing a corner results in the inversion of the design. When this happens a 'side reverse' must be used to restore the pattern so that it approaches the next corner as before. A mirror standing vertically on the pattern or lace at right angles to the footside, this time along a row of points, not between them, will show a possible design (figures 115 and 116). Move the

mirror along the lace and note that there are several possible side reverses for this design.

When a zig-zag trail is examined closely it can be seen that when it travels to one side there is one more pair of passives than when it travels towards the other side. It follows that when a side reverse is made the thicker 'leg' of the trail will still travel in the same direction, i.e. to the left or right,

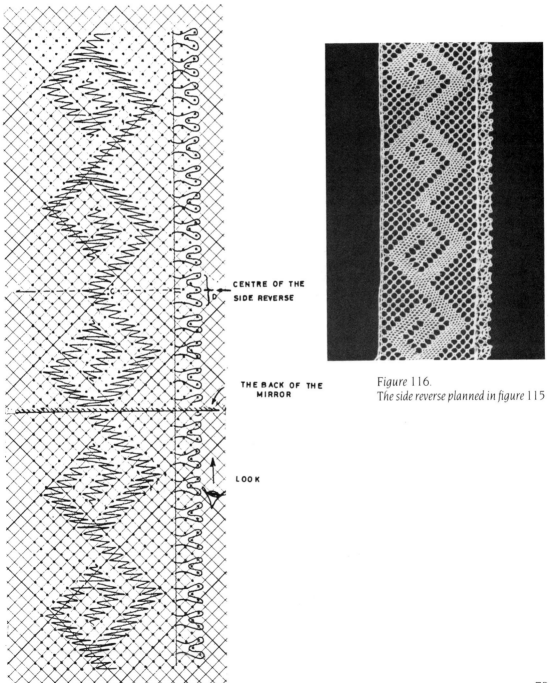

CENTRE OF THE
SIDE REVERSE

THE BACK OF THE
MIRROR

LOOK

Figure 115.
A *pricking showing the position of a mirror for planning a side reverse together with the side reverse it illustrates*

Figure 116.
The side reverse planned in figure 115

73

whereas it would be aesthetically more correct for it to change sides. To accomplish this an extra pinhole is required as the trail changes direction at the centre point of the reverse *C*. Most trails can be kept to an even density by using an extra pinhole every time it changes direction. If a trail looks thin and starved an extra pair can be introduced to improve its appearance. In this pattern an extra pair has been included in the continuous section of the trail but not in the 'curl'. Although the border does not vary when inverted the remainder of the pattern determines the point at which the side reverse occurs, causing the points of the border to become 'out of step' by the time the next corner is reached. Hence the border must be modified at point *D*.

NON-REVERSING CORNER (figures 117 and 118)
A pattern that reverses its direction when inverted can be cornered without this reversal occurring. This time a mirror is not used, instead make a tracing of the main features of the pattern and, without turning it over, place it at right angles to the original with the ends overlapping. Adjust the position of the overlap until a possible corner is found. The design may require adapting so that the two sections of the pattern flow one into the other and conform to the rules and limitations imposed by the corner itself.

Figure 118.
The non-reversing corner planned in figure 117

Figure 117.
Planning a non-reversing corner using a tracing ▶

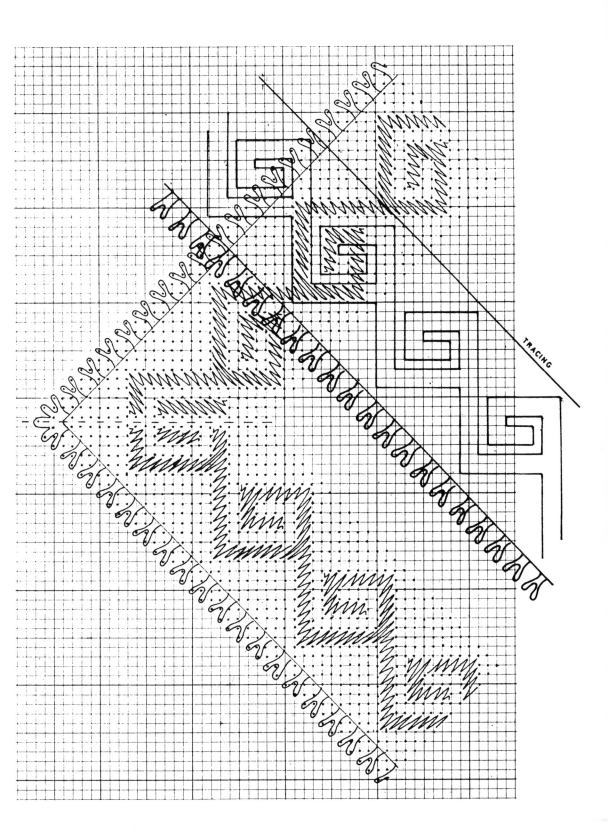

TRACING

75

CORNER WITH FANS ALONG THE INNER EDGE
(figures 119 and 120)
Corners can be turned with the footside on the outer edge
e.g. for the inner edge of a square neckline.

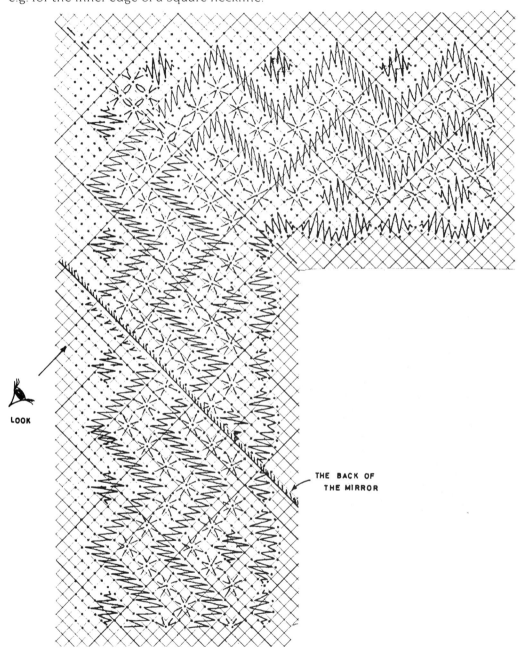

LOOK

THE BACK OF
THE MIRROR

Figure 119.
A pricking showing the position of the
mirror when planning a corner with
the fans along the inner edge

Figure 120.
The corner with fans along the inner
edge planned in figure 119

Figure 121.
A pricking for a runner end

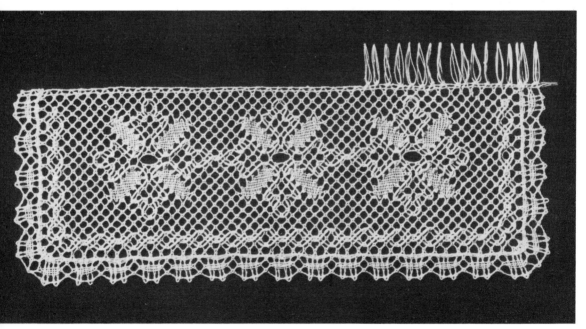

Figure 122.
The runner end made on pricking above

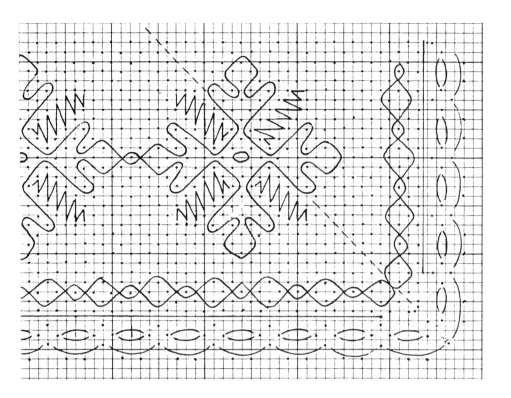

RUNNER END (figures 121-122)

Sometimes a lace edging is required for the end of a runner or stole with a finished edge at both ends. This can be achieved by starting the lace along the material/lace junction, (a mock footside), going straight into a corner and changing direction. Work along the edging and finish, after cornering again, along the material/lace junction (another mock footside) (figure 123).

This runner end has been worked with the corner part-way through the motif of the design since this motif could not be worked satisfactorily with the corner passing through its centre, and if the corner was worked after the motif there would be too large an area of plain torchon ground.

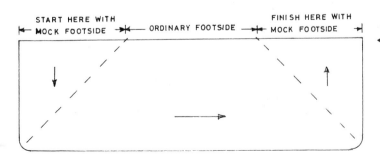

START HERE WITH ⊢← MOCK FOOTSIDE →⊩←— ORDINARY FOOTSIDE —⊩ FINISH HERE WITH MOCK FOOTSIDE —⊣

◀ Figure 123.
Working directions for the runner end (figures 121 and 122)

HANDKERCHIEF CORNER (figures 124-127)

Triangles are frequently used to decorate the corners of handkerchiefs or serviettes and they are, themselves, taken from corners of edgings. To adapt an edging to produce one of these corners place a piece of paper on the lace, or pattern with its edge at 45 degrees to the footside and stand a mirror on the lace and paper as before. The paper and mirror should cross each other at right angles. Move the mirror along the lace to find a suitable corner. If the lace is too narrow and does not fill the corner use torchon ground or, if there is a large space, try using motifs from the pattern to complete the triangle. When the pattern for this corner was drawn diagonally on 2mm squared paper it looked rather small so another row of spiders was added along the headside and more diamonds of half stitch introduced into the open space in the centre of the design.

A handkerchief or serviette with a lace corner may look unfinished. A better effect is produced if a narrow edging of lace is made around the remainder of the material. Ideas for an extended corner can be found if the paper covering the lace or pattern is folded back to expose the headside when the corner is being designed.

Note that this corner has been designed with the corner occurring along a row of points. When the lace is made a pair of bobbins is added at each point from *A-B*. Another pair is added at point *C* to work the centre row of the corner and taken out at *D* the end of the row. Pairs are left out at the end of each following row to *E*. There are several methods for finishing off. In this case the ends would be sewn into the hem of the article.

Figure 124.
A pricking showing the position of a
mirror and a paper mask when
planning an extended handkerchief
corner

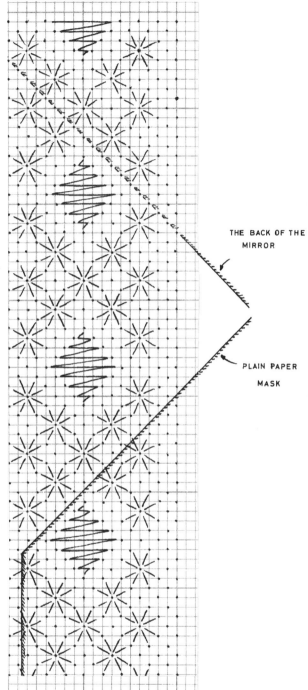

THE BACK OF THE
MIRROR

PLAIN PAPER

MASK

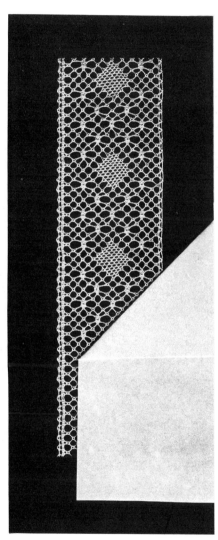

Figure 125.
The lace worked on pricking figure
124 with its paper mask

81

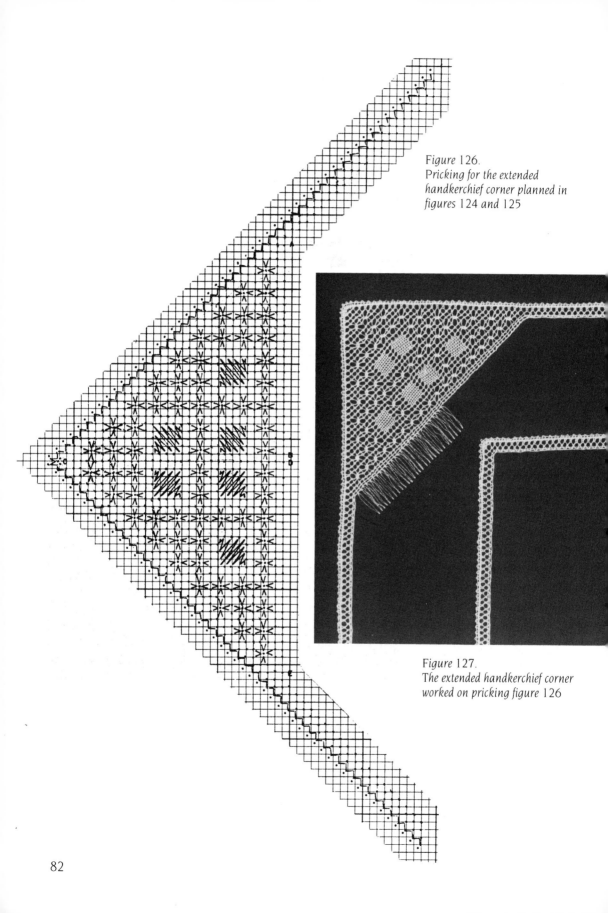

Figure 126.
Pricking for the extended
handkerchief corner planned in
figures 124 and 125

Figure 127.
The extended handkerchief corner
worked on pricking figure 126

82

PAPERWEIGHTS (figures 128-131)

A paperweight motif may be designed by placing a mirror across the corner of a piece of lace or pattern and looking for possible designs. Because of their small size these items require fine threads and are drawn as an edging pattern plotted diagonally across the paper.

Figure 128.
A pricking of an edging showing the position of the mirror when planning a paperweight motif

Figure 129.
Lace worked on pricking figure 128

LOOK

THE BACK OF THE MIRROR

Figure 130.
Pricking of the paperweight motif
planned in figures 128 and 129

Figure 131.
The paperweight motif worked on
pricking figure 130

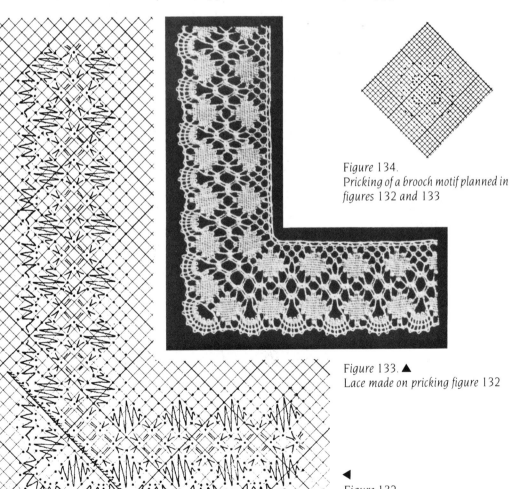

Figure 134.
Pricking of a brooch motif planned in
figures 132 and 133

Figure 133. ▲
Lace made on pricking figure 132

◄

Figure 132.
A pricking showing how brooch
motifs can be planned from corners

THE BACK OF THE
MIRROR

LOOK

BROOCHES (figures 132-141)

These designs are drawn diagonally across 1mm graph paper requiring a 120-160 Honiton thread for making the lace, and can be developed along the lines of the paperweight motif (figures 132-135). Alternatively the designs may be taken from a straight section of the lace. Finish these items by tying reef knots and sewing all the ends through the backing (figures 136-141).

Figure 137.
The lace made on pricking figure 136

Figure 135.
Brooch motif worked in 120 Honiton thread on pricking figure 134

SECTION TO BE USED
FOR THE SQUARE
BROOCH MOTIF

SECTION TO BE USED
FOR THE OVAL
BROOCH MOTIF

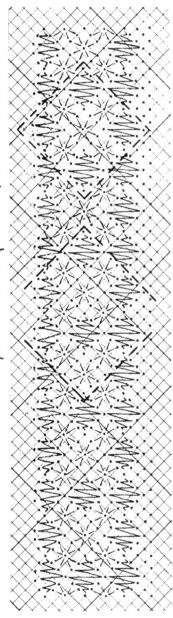

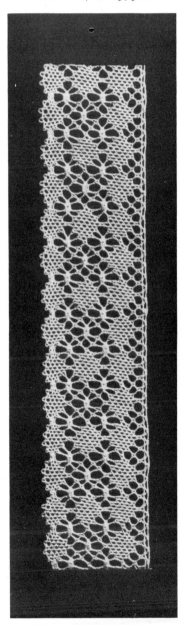

Figure 136.
Pricking showing how brooch motifs can be planned from straight pieces of lace

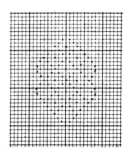

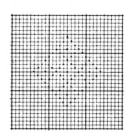

Figure 138.
The pricking for an oval brooch motif planned in figures 136 and 137

Figure 140.
Pricking for a square brooch motif planned from figures 136 and 137

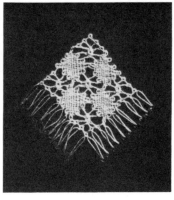

Figure 139.
An oval brooch motif worked in 180 Honiton thread worked on pricking figure 138

Figure 141.
A square brooch motif worked in 180 Honiton thread on pricking figure 140. The diamonds are worked in whole stitch instead of half stitch

Figure 142.
A pricking showing the position of a mirror when planning a square mat

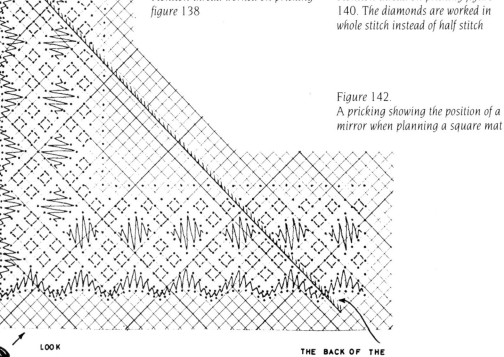

LOOK

THE BACK OF THE MIRROR

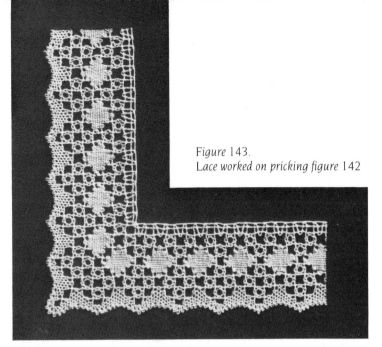

Figure 143.
Lace worked on pricking figure 142

Figure 144.
The pricking for a square mat
planned in figures 142 and 143

Figure 145.
The lace mat made on pricking figure
144

SQUARE MATS (figures 142-145)
Designs for mats can be developed by placing the mirror in
a suitable position across a lace or pattern corner and
developing the vacant space between the design and the
mirror. For this mat two diamonds of whole stitch and one
of rose ground could have been used instead of the heart-
shaped whole stitch section. Note that a point has been
omitted at the dip of the heart and a line of twists made with
the passives.

Before copying the mat draw the two lines of dashes
crossing at right angles that represent the lines through the
corners. Start by plotting the motifs in the centre, i.e. the
hearts, and check that they meet correctly before moving
further out. Next plot the whole stitch diamonds, again

check that they meet correctly before filling the areas of rose ground and finishing with the fans. This mat, drawn straight on the graph paper, was developed from the narrow edging drawn diagonally across the paper. As the two thicknesses of thread work-up slightly differently on their respective scales the indented fans of the mat required one more pair of passives than the fans of the fine edging.

RECTANGULAR MATS (figures 146-150)
These can be developed from square mats or edgings. Rectangular mats can be worked in one direction starting at one end and finishing at the other or in four with a seam through the centre. The pins along the centre seam are slightly offset and twisted pairs are taken around these pins when working in one direction and sewings taken in their loops when working in the opposite direction.

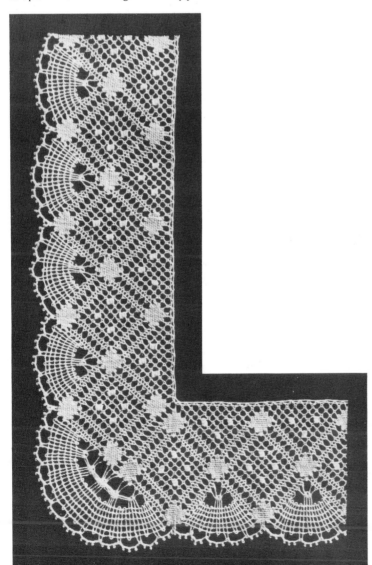

Figure 146.
Lace made on pricking 147

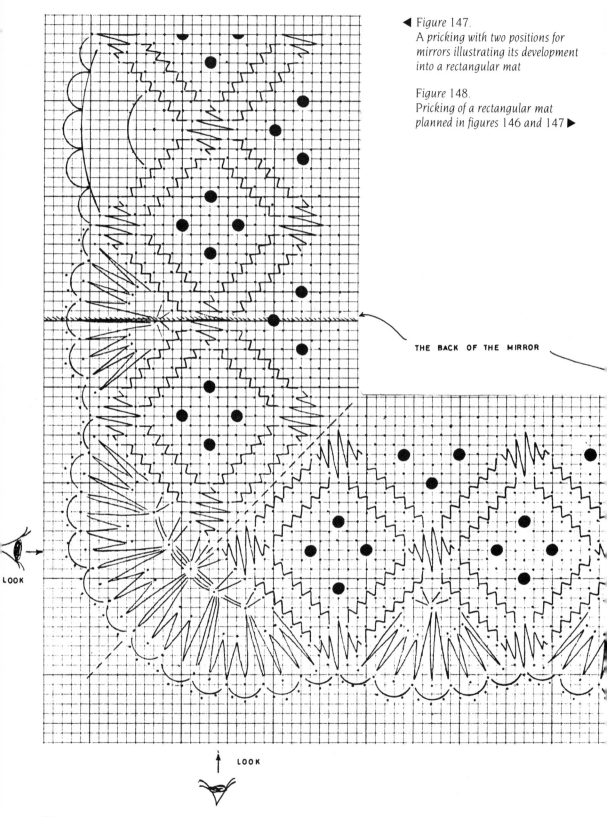

◄ Figure 147.
A pricking with two positions for
mirrors illustrating its development
into a rectangular mat

Figure 148.
Pricking of a rectangular mat
planned in figures 146 and 147 ▶

THE BACK OF THE MIRROR

LOOK

LOOK

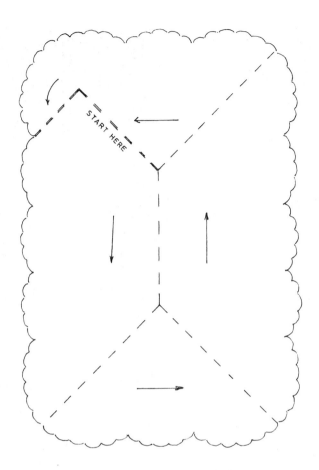

START HERE

Figure 149.
Working directions for a rectangular
mat made on pricking figure 148

◀ Figure 150.
A rectangular mat made on pricking
figure 148

BOOKMARKS AND INSERTIONS (figures 151-6)
A mirror placed on a line of pins along the lace or pattern
will show designs that may be useful for bookmarks or
insertions depending on which way the mirror faces. Adapt
the sides of the pattern to produce a suitable beginning for
the bookmark. Note that the whole stitch trail of the original
edging has been changed to half stitch in the insertion.

Figure 151.
A *pricking showing the positions of
the mirror when planning an
insertion or bookmark*
▼

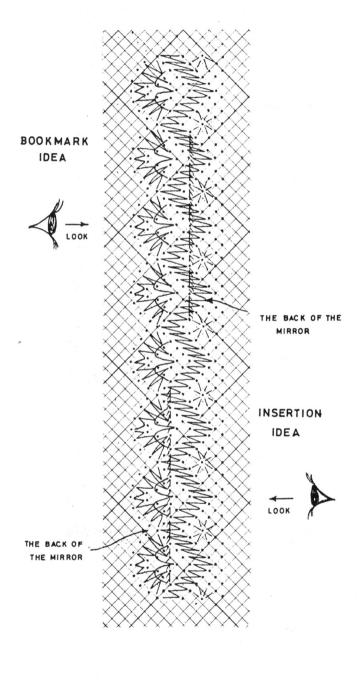

BOOKMARK
IDEA

LOOK

THE BACK OF THE
MIRROR

INSERTION
IDEA

LOOK

THE BACK OF
THE MIRROR

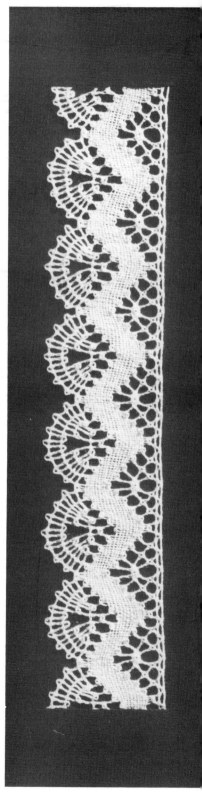

Figure 152.
Lace made on pricking figure 151▶

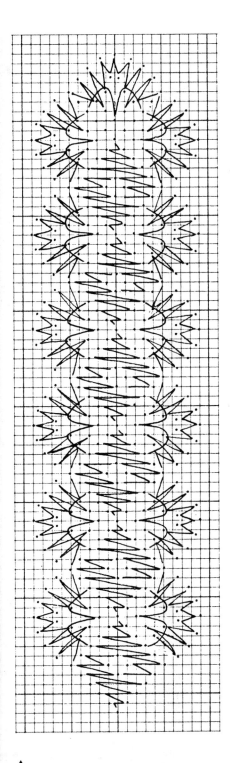

Figure 153.
Pricking of the bookmark planned in
figures 151 and 152

Figure 154.
The bookmark made on pricking
figure 153
▼

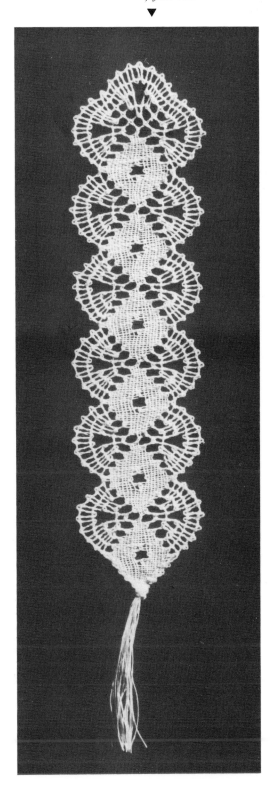

Figure 155.
Pricking of an insertion planned in
figures 151 and 152

Figure 156.
The insertion made on pricking
figure 155 ▶

ITEMS MADE IN SEVERAL PIECES (figures 157-163)
Once mats, insertions and edgings can be designed to complement each other larger items can be built up. A tablecloth can start as a square mat surrounded by a series of insertions and finished with an edging (figure 157). The successive pieces are oversewn together through the footside pinholes therefore ensuring that there is the same number of holes along the edge of both pieces. Designing a tablecloth usually starts with the central mat (figure 158). Motifs taken from this mat may be enlarged or otherwise adapted and used for the first insertion (figure 160). In this case the same design was used for the second insertion but the design could have been further adapted if required. The third insertion is essentially a section lifted directly from the central mat with the repetitive gimp border added to the upper edge (figures 161 and 162). Try standing mirrors on the mat facing each other; the design can be seen if they are tilted correctly. A border (figure 163) was designed to complement the whole.

Figure 157.
Plan of the tablecloth sections

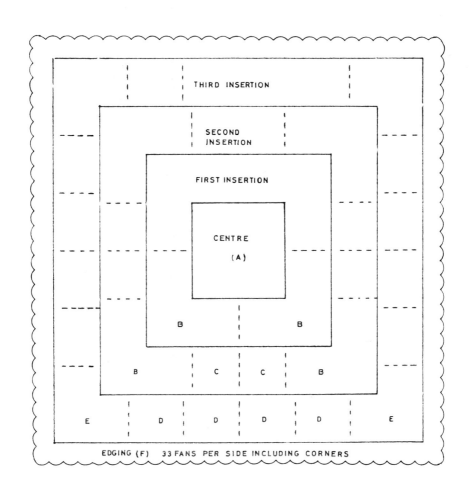

EDGING (F)   33 FANS PER SIDE INCLUDING CORNERS

Figure 158.
The tablecloth centre (pricking)

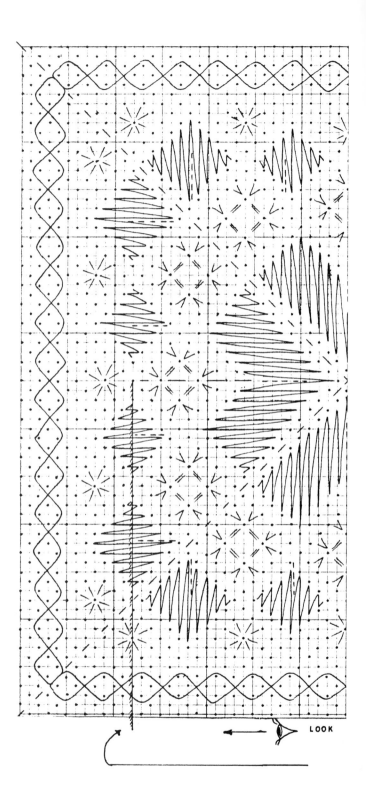

LOOK

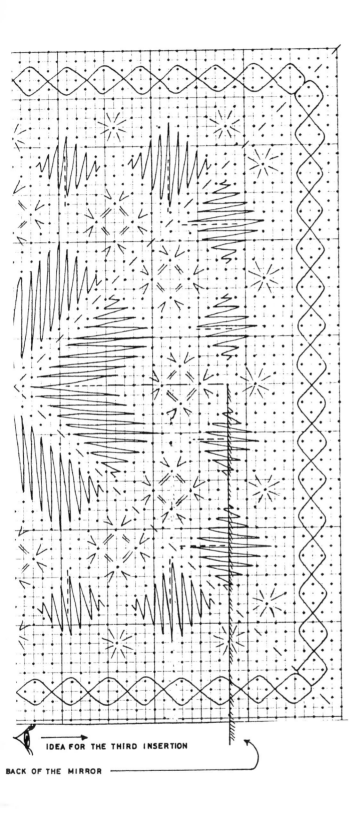

IDEA FOR THE THIRD INSERTION

BACK OF THE MIRROR

99

Figure 159.
A tablecloth made in several sections

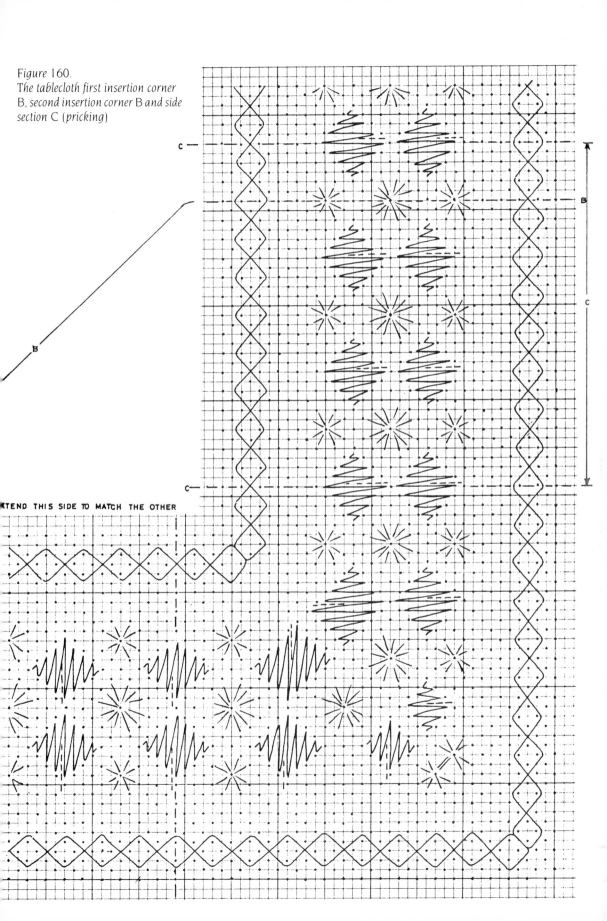

Figure 160.
The tablecloth first insertion corner
B, second insertion corner B and side
section C (*pricking*)

EXTEND THIS SIDE TO MATCH THE OTHER

Figure 161.
The tablecloth third insertion, side section D (pricking). The gimp follows the dotted line for alternate sections (pricking)

When copying these patterns check the number of points along the sides of the diamonds, most have five or six points per side. One corner involves a diamond of four points per side and a rectangle with sides of five and six points. This was necessary for negotiating the corner. Also check the number of legs per side for the spiders. Some have two legs per side others three.

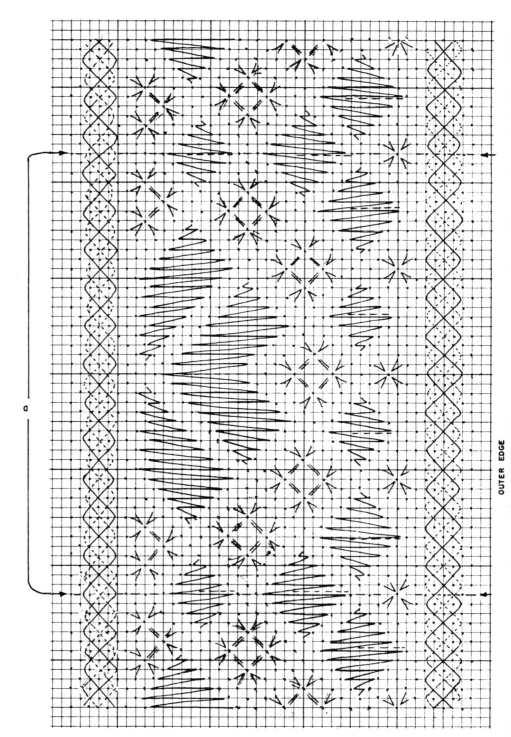

a

OUTER EDGE

Figure 162.
The tablecloth third insertion, corner
E (pricking). The gimp follows the
dotted line for alternate corners

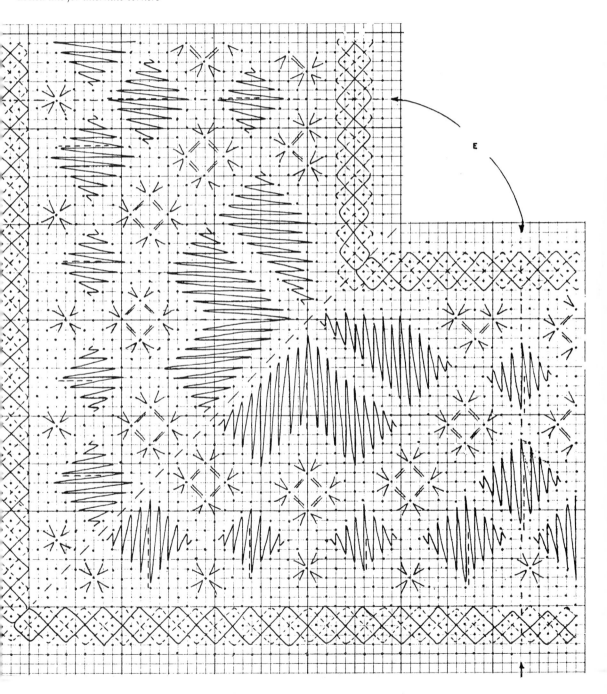

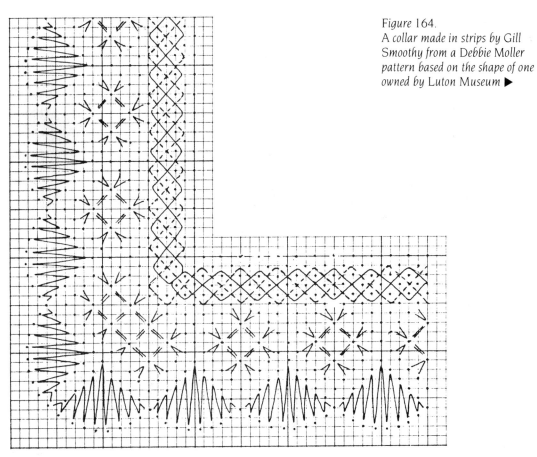

Figure 164.
A collar made in strips by Gill
Smoothy from a Debbie Moller
pattern based on the shape of one
owned by Luton Museum ▶

Figure 163.
The tablecloth edging F (pricking).
The gimp follows the dotted line for
alternate corners

Other items can be made in strips and oversewn together.
The copy of the Victorian collar in Luton Museum was
specifically designed to show that, with application and
minimal sewing skills, lacemakers with very little knowledge
and experience can produce quite spectacular pieces of
work. This collar was made in separate strips oversewn
together and with some joins neatened and strengthened
with silk binding (figure 164).

Designs for collars and other clothing start with simple
dressmakers' paper patterns suitably enlarged to allow for
shrinkage. This pattern can be divided into strips if required
and lace patterns designed to fit the individual sections;
strips may be made longer and cut to length if preferred.
Finally the strips are joined together, normally by
oversewing, using the footside holes where appropriate.
Neaten and strengthen seams with a fine binding if
required.

10.
Freestyle Pictures

EDWARDIAN LADY

Freestyle pictures can be worked within the framework of torchon ground. Such a picture starts as a simple tracing where most of the enclosed spaces are sufficiently large to show clearly in the finished lace and the areas of whole and half stitch not so large that they become impractical to work and uninteresting to look at. (The dress's train is rather large but it would be difficult to bring in variation successfully.) Other areas such as the lady's collar, cuff and hand are rather small but such details may be necessary for a meaningful picture and are eyecatching if successfully worked. (The collar was more successful than the hand and cuff.)

Once a suitable tracing has been made (children's painting books and embroidery designs are useful sources) the scale of work and thread must be chosen and the stitches for the enclosed areas selected. Although at first the scale of the pricking may seem rather small this is necessary for there to be sufficient threads entering and leaving the enclosed spaces for smooth curves and details to be made. As there was a large expanse of background it required variation. This was achieved by surrounding the main design with a larger simplified silhouette and working contrasting grounds within and without this boundary.

Three main contrasting stitches were used – half stitch, torchon ground and rose ground, with details worked in whole stitch and whole stitch and twist. A single motif of rose ground was introduced into the centre of the hat to add interest, which it does successfully.

The next stage is to transfer the tracing to the graph paper. Temporarily secure the two together with paper clips or Blu-Tack. Examine the boundaries of the enclosed spaces noting how the lace could be worked on the different sides. Adjust the position of the design over the squares as required so that the lace can be made successfully along the boundaries. Of course not all the boundaries can be placed in ideal positions, in fact very few can. Sometimes the lines of the tracing can be adjusted slightly, otherwise the answer is compromise.

Figure 165.
An Edwardian lady, a freestyle design ▶

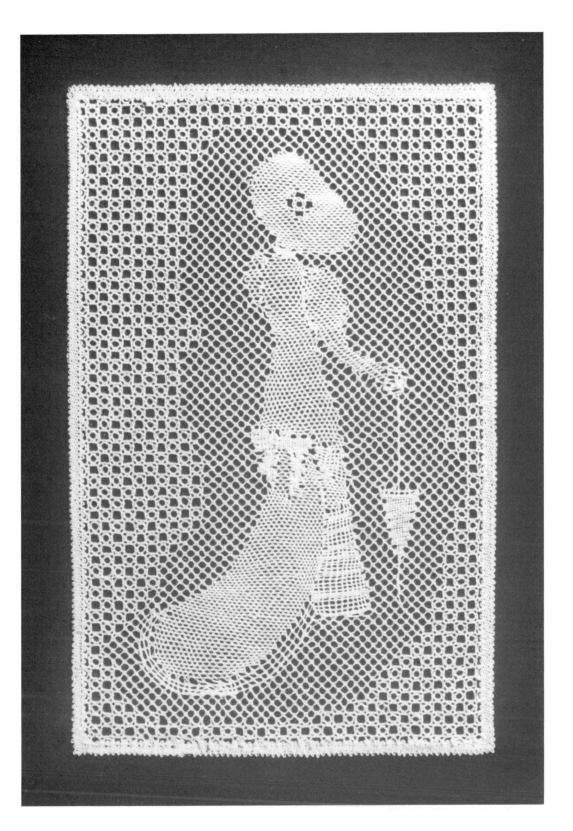

Figure 166.
An Edwardian lady, preparation of
the pricking

Once the best position for the tracing has been established a piece of carbon paper can be placed beneath it and the design transferred to the graph paper. The design and position of the braid frame can be decided and drawn next.

The pinholes along the borders of the enclosed spaces are not marked on the graph paper. Instead the graph paper is placed over the pricking card and all the lines transferred to the card with non-smudge carbon paper. The braid frame is pricked first then the grounds with the ground surrounding the lady pricked across the enclosed spaces of the design. Ink the lines of the design and silhouette and start making the lace. The braid frame of this piece was worked first and the picture started from the top. As the design was reached pinholes were made along the borders of the enclosed spaces where the pairs of the background would enter or leave the different sections. Sometimes, and ideally, a hole would already be there otherwise it is a case of 'make a hole when you need one'. The place where a row of holes crosses the line may be a suitable position for a pin. A pencil-shaped pricker is better than a fat one at this stage. The hat (figure 167) has been drawn in detail to illustrate the relationship between the holes along its outer edge, the holes of the ground and the requirements of the half stitch. Where possible the holes are situated on the lines of the graph paper which, in this case, indicate the positions of the pairs entering or leaving the half stitch. The workers of the half stitch areas were kept horizontal throughout but as the hat progressed it became more open and looked starved. One way of combatting this problem is to add more pairs or, as here, extra rows can be worked. This was a convenient

Figure 167.
Detail of the Edwardian lady's hat

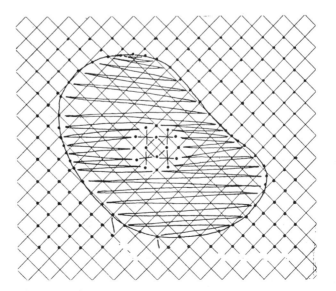

solution as it fitted in well with the requirements of the rose ground motif in the centre. The number of holes around this motif was determined by the requirements of the workers on either side.

Keep the graph paper pricking handy as solutions to problems like this can often be solved by sketching pairs and pinholes before working the rows and having to undo. Positioning the holes along the boundaries is a skill that develops with practice and as much, or more, is learnt when making the lace as by drawing the pricking. Be prepared to meet snags. The fun of making these pictures is meeting and solving the problems and making the picture work in spite of the difficulties.

Few extra pairs were required in making this picture and those added were mainly for the train border where the pairs follow the line of the design rather than their more usual routes.

TOADSTOOLS (figures 168 and 169)
This picture started as a simple tracing, transferred to graph paper in the usual way and the design and position of the frame braid determined. Five areas are quite large, too large for plain whole or half stitch but suitable for fancy filling stitches. Three were selected to contain filling stitches, the other two to have whole and half stitch broken into interesting and manageable sections. The areas within the three shapes destined to contain fillings were cut away. Two filling stitches compatible with the subject of the picture and size of the vacant shape were selected from one of the specialist books and plotted on separate pieces of paper. The main design was placed over each filling in turn. The intention this time was to use the filling at an angle that would complement the design. Each was adjusted to the best position as regards its angle to the outline of the space and the pinholes near the border and secured in position with cellophane tape. The area of the lower left toadstool was replaced with plain paper. The filling of whole stitch bars separated by tallies was drawn freehand to fill the space. The division lines of the whole and half stitch toadstools were drawn in.

As before the graph paper was placed over the card, the design transferred to the card and the grounds, fillings and frame braid pricked. This time the pricking of the ground was not continued across the design. The same order of work was followed, however this time no attempt was made to keep the whole and half stitch workers horizontal, on the contrary the direction of these and the passives was used to complement the design. The unusual angles of the different areas caused many extra pairs to be needed.

Pictures rarely turn out exactly as imagined, sometimes even better. Do not expect everything to work perfectly the first time, after all the lace designers of the past used to serve many years apprenticeship before they could consider themselves true designers.

Figure 168.
Toadstools, a freestyle design based on a sketch by Eunice Kirk

Figure 169
Toadstools, preparation of the pricking ▶

11.
Circular Lace

Circular edgings and mats can be successfully drawn on polar co-ordinate paper. This paper consists of a series of circles crossed by straight radial lines.

NARROW CIRCULAR EDGING (figures 170 and 171)
Torchon ground can sometimes be plotted on polar co-ordinate paper in the same manner as on squared graph paper. The footside for this edging lies along one of the circles with points marked where alternate radial lines cross it. The points of the ground are plotted diagonally across the squares for the width required. Half stitch is often more successful than whole stitch for curved lace as it adapts more easily to the 'spreading' effect. More pairs may be added to the fan to compensate for its increased area.

Figure 170.
A circular edging made on pricking figure 171 using DMC Retors d'Alsace thread No. 30, *gimp* DMC *Perle No. 8*

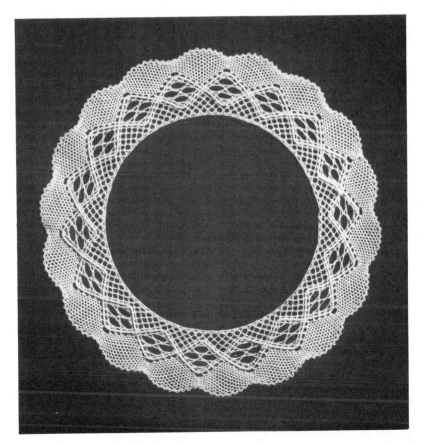

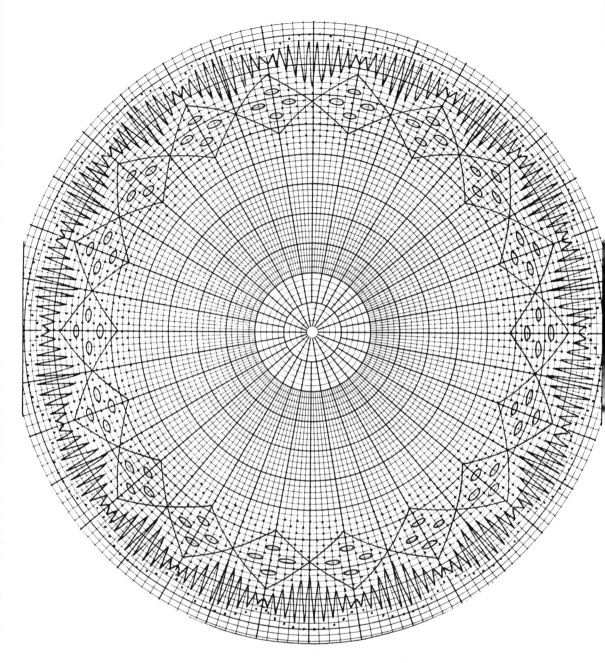

Figure 171.
A circular edging (pricking)

WORKING OUT GRIDS (figure 172)
Sometimes the spacing of the radial lines does not match
that of the circles. When this happens suitable positions can
still be found for the points. Start by deciding the size of the
'diamond' of the torchon ground and plot a couple of rows
of points on squared paper. Offer the squared paper up to a
radial line on the polar co-ordinate paper (position I) and
choose circles corresponding to the spacing of the points on
the squared paper. In the outer band of the example,
alternate lines, from points A, of the squared paper

correspond to every fifth circle, so plot points *1, 2, 3,* etc. along the radial line according to this spacing. Next estimate the spacing of the points around these circles by offering the squared graph paper up to one of them (position II). Here the alternate lines from points *C* of the squared paper match every radial line crossing the circle, plot points *4, 5, 6,* etc. Plot a small section with points at every intersection along the selected circles. Return the squared graph paper to position I and estimate where the intermediate lines from point *B* meet the radial line on the polar co-ordinate paper; mid-way between the circles occupied by the previous points. Return the squared graph paper to position II and here the intermediate lines from point *D* occur mid-way between the radial lines. Plot the intermediate points *7, 8, 9,* etc. mid-way between the circles already occupied by points and mid-way between the radial lines. These points are easily plotted in by eye. However, lightly sketched lines linking the easily plotted points helps to position the intermediate points. If the squared paper is offered up to a circle of the polar co-ordinate paper closer to the centre (position III) a different scale occurs. (Compare the scales of the two graph papers at the point where they meet only.) For the inner band the alternate lines from points *E* on the squared graph paper correspond to positions that are one and a half spaces between the radial lines points *4, 5, 6,* etc. The spacing along the radial lines is the same, i.e. alternate lines correspond to every fifth circle points *1, 2, 3,* etc. and the intermediate lines correspond to the space half way between them. The intermediate points *7, 8, 9,* etc. are best plotted by eye although their positions can be calculated accurately if required.

Figure 172.
Working out grids on polar co-ordinate paper

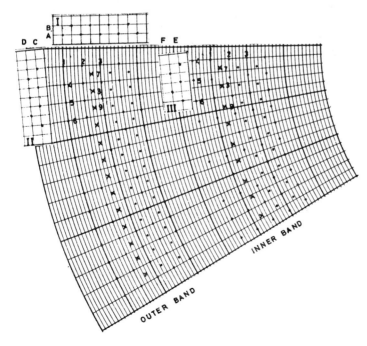

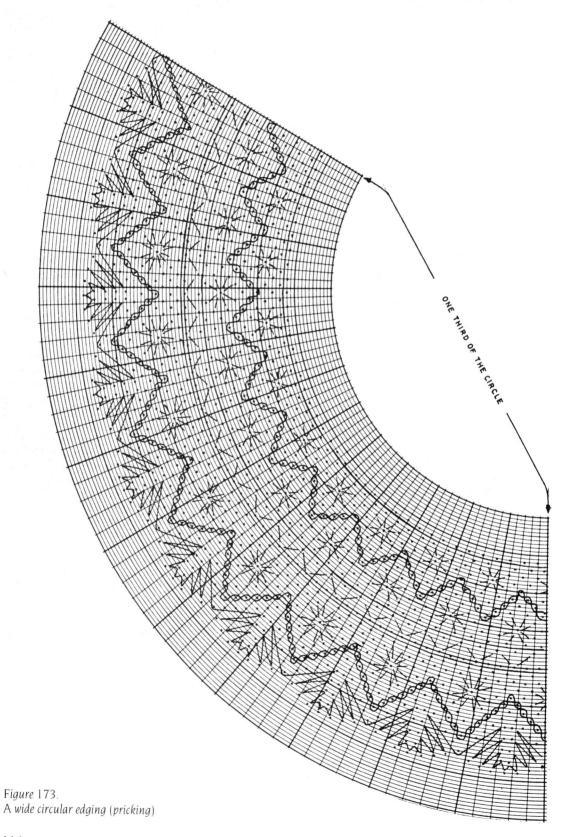

ONE THIRD OF THE CIRCLE

Figure 173.
A wide circular edging (pricking)

116

Figure 174.
A *wide circular edging made on pricking figure 173 using Bockens No. 80 linen thread, gimp DMC Perle No. 8*

WIDER EDGINGS (figures 173 and 174)
As a circular edging becomes wider the radial lines crossing the circles spread, the squares become rectangles and eventually distortion of the torchon ground becomes unacceptable. However, wider edgings can be made if the band is 'broken' at certain distances from the centre so that the size and shape of the ground can be recovered. The wide edging is essentially a series of separate bands connected at regular intervals. In this case alternate pins of the inner band correspond to every third pin of the outer band. The bands can be joined by using a 'zig-zag' of plaits or leaves, kisses, or workers may make 'whole stitch, pin, whole stitch' and return to their own bands.

CIRCULAR MAT (figures 175 and 176)
This circular mat consists of two bands of whole stitch triangles and French fans separated by a ring of half stitch. The side of the triangle lying along one of the circles of the paper is reduced in length compared with one drawn on

squared paper and will not work up satisfactorily if plotted in the usual way. To compensate for this the number of points along this circle are reduced so that all are used by the time the widest part of the triangle has been reached, the triangle is now complete. The fan is worked using the passives as they pass out from the longest line of whole stitch of the triangle.

Torchon ground cannot be worked very close to the centre of a circle, the distortion is too great, so this part of the mat has been filled with plaits and leaves. The fans of the inner ring are slightly distorted along the three points where they meet the half stitch circle.

To compensate for the 'spreading' effect the inner edge of the outer band of fans and triangles has five pins to every four of the half stitch band. The two are joined together using kisses at the two centre pins of the triangles where the points of the two sections coincide. Between these joining points there are two points along the half stitch band and three along the triangle edge.

Figure 175.
A circular mat made on pricking
figure 176 using DMC Retors
d'Alsace thread No. 30

Figure 176.
A circular mat (pricking)

COLLAR (figures 177 and 178)

The first stage in making any collar is a dressmakers' paper pattern (excluding seam allowance) of the required size and shape. The lace pattern should be a little larger than the paper pattern as lace shrinks when washed. Most authorities quote an allowance of $1/15$ but I have one piece worked in No. 35 linen that shrank by $1/10$. I have also found that the finer threads and more open designs shrink less. The shrinkage is caused more by the release of tension in the fabric than the shortening of the threads. Thus lace worked with a strong tension will shrink more than that worked loosely.

When old lace collars are examined many are found to have a narrow whole stitch band along the neckline extending as a small 'tab' at each end. These tabs are turned in and stitched to the band for strengthening; collars without these reinforced corners weaken quickly at these points. A strong band along the neckline, whether plain whole stitch or not, is necessary to take the wear and tear of sewing it to and removing it from garments as well as the general wear it will receive. This band is often tucked inside

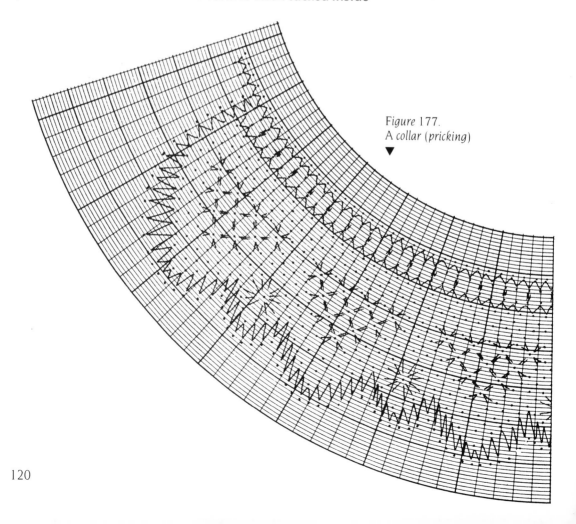

Figure 177.
A collar (pricking)
▼

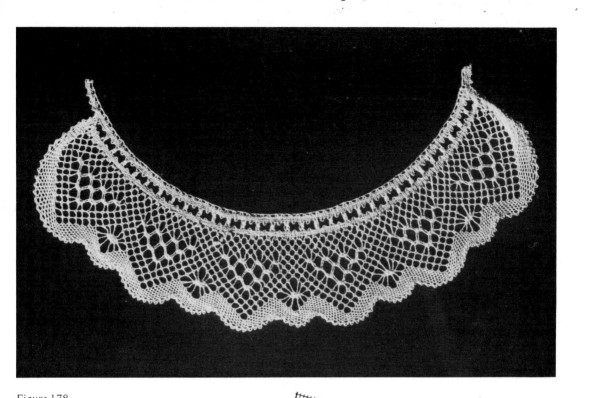

Figure 178.
A collar made on pricking figure 177
using Bockens No. 80 linen thread

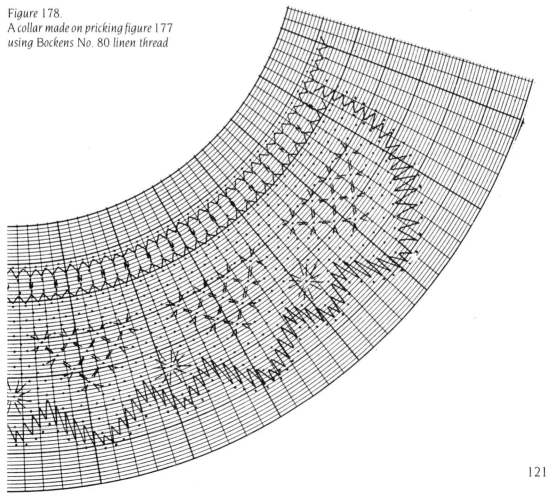

the neckline of the garment and attached there. However, since neckline bands like the one shown are shorter than the rest of the collar they may cause the collar to pucker if folded inside the garment neckline. I prefer a bias strip sewn to the collar for this purpose.

When designing a torchon collar place the dressmakers' paper pattern (excluding seam allowance but including allowance for shrinkage) on polar co-ordinate paper and choose circles to be its inner and outer boundaries. Also lightly sketch the positions of the two ends of the collar. Decide on the scale of work and sketch a small section of grid, then start working on the design; probably one already prepared on squared paper. When the design has been drawn check that it fits satisfactorily into its allotted place and that there is sufficient room for the ends. If the collar is to have square ends they may be plotted and worked as a runner end. In this example the half stitch trail started at the beginning of the neck edge and was worked outwards at right angles. Pairs necessary for the increasing width of the trail, the second whole stitch braid and the torchon ground were added as required until the trail started to decrease in width, when pairs for the torchon ground were left out of the trail as usual. To finish the collar pairs were taken out of the half stitch trail as required. The two tabs should be neatly folded back and stitched securely in place.

FREESTYLE FAN (frontispiece and figure 179a-c)
This fan was designed following a similar sequence to that used for the Edwardian lady. Suitable designs can be taken from embroidery patterns, children's painting books, etc. Photocopiers that increase or decrease scale are very useful for bringing the original to a suitable size. Trace different parts of the design onto separate pieces of paper and arrange them into a pleasing picture. Tape them onto a piece of tracing paper and use carbon paper to transfer the design onto graph paper. This design was carefully modified to break the ground from one end of the fan to the other thus enabling the scale to be changed. The design was then colour coded. Whole stitch areas were coloured red with felt tip pen, half stitch yellow and the gimps were drawn in black. Any large areas show up well in colour and judicious use of Tipp-Ex allows alterations to be made as required. The pricking was prepared as for the Edwardian lady and the pinholes along the curves altered as required when the lace was made. An alternative symbol was used to indicate rose ground namely a cross in the centre of each 'rose'.

Figure 179A.
A fan (pricking section A)

Key

half stitch (coloured
yellow on my pattern)

whole stitch (coloured
red on my pattern)

Figure 179B
A fan (pricking section B)

Figure 179C.
A fan (pricking section C)

12.
Ovals and Ellipses

SIMPLE OVAL EDGING
The simplest method of designing an oval edging is to draw a circular one with a matching straight edging. The polar coordinate paper used here has concentric circles at every 1/16-inch and the matching edging was worked on 1/16-inch squared graph paper. The circle was cut in half so that the fans are complete or halved; this particular design shows both. Three pattern repeats of the straight edging have been introduced on either side between the semi-circles, one side having three complete fans and the other two complete fans

Figure 180
An oval edging (pricking) ▶

Figure 181.
An oval edging made on pricking figure 180 using DMC Retors d'Alsace thread No. 30

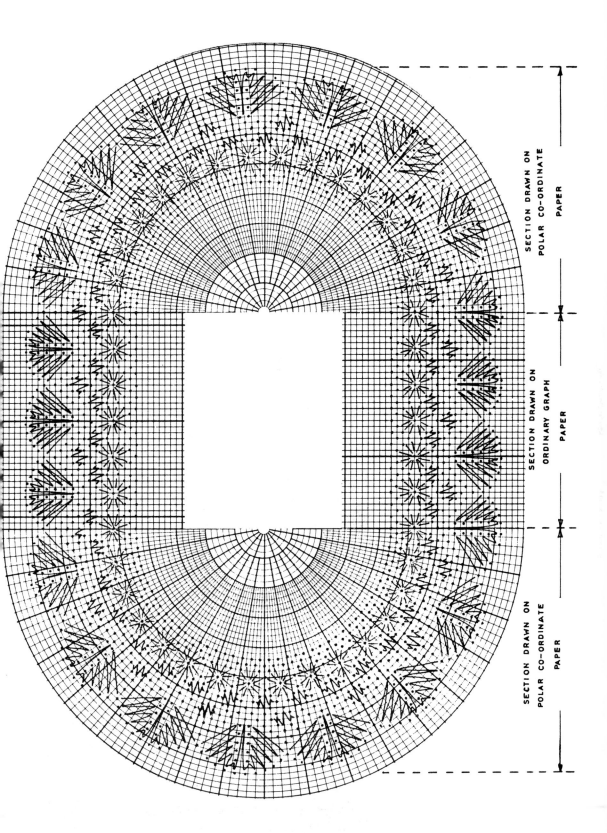

SECTION DRAWN ON
POLAR CO-ORDINATE
PAPER

SECTION DRAWN ON
ORDINARY GRAPH
PAPER

SECTION DRAWN ON
POLAR CO-ORDINATE
PAPER

127

and a 'half fan' at each end. The four pieces were secured together with cellophane tape before pricking.

This method does not produce a true ellipse but has the advantage of being easier.

AN ELLIPSE (figures 182-7)
For a true ellipse use 1mm squared graph paper and draw two circles from the same centre point. One has a diameter the length of the ellipse and the other a diameter the width of the ellipse (figure 182). Draw two lines crossing at right angles through the centre point so that one passes through its length *L-L* and the other through its width *W-W*. Draw at least three radial lines, well spaced, from the centre point to the outer circle in each of the four sections; the exact positions of these lines is not important. *Find point *A*

Figure 182.
Drawing an ellipse

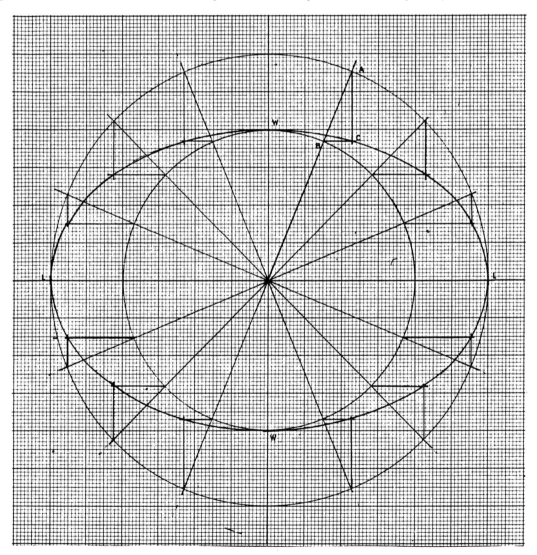

where a radial line crosses the outer circle and draw a line from here parallel to line *W-W*, i.e. follow a graph line towards line *L-L*. Find point *B* where the same radial line crosses the smaller circle and draw a line from here parallel to line *L-L*, i.e. follow a graph line away from line *W-W*. These two lines cross at point *C*. Repeat from * for as many radial lines as you wish to draw. The curve of the ellipse passes through all points *C*. This curve can be drawn free-hand, using French curves or a flexi-curve. French curves are used by offering each part of its many curves up to the points and, by trial and error, finding the section that gives the best line between two or three points. Draw in the line and move on to the next section. A flexi-curve can be bent to follow the points and a line can be drawn along its edge. As the construction lines are confusing it is helpful if the ellipse is traced and the following drawing carried out on the tracing. Place a flexi-curve or piece of string along the ellipse and mark the ends of one quarter *P-Q* (figure 183). Straighten out the flexi-curve or string and measure its length. Prepare the

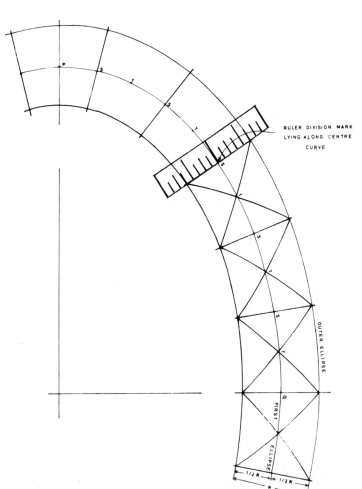

Figure 183.
The next stage in drawn an elliptical edging using one quarter of the ellipse ▶

RULER DIVISION MARK
LYING ALONG CENTRE
CURVE

OUTER ELLIPSE

FIRST ELLIPSE

Figure 184.
Drawing the grid for an elliptical edging
▼

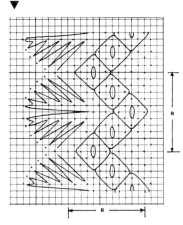

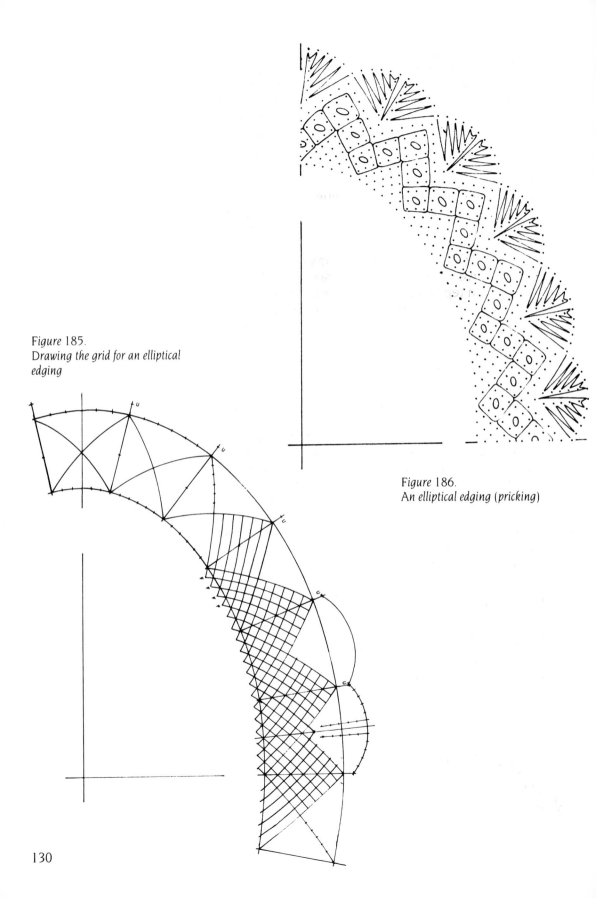

Figure 185.
Drawing the grid for an elliptical
edging

Figure 186.
An elliptical edging (pricking)

pattern to scale on squared paper and measure the length of one pattern repeat R (figure 184). Calculate the number of pattern repeats that will fit along the length P-Q (figure 183) and mark their positions S. (Mine fitted approximately five and a half times.) Draw the dividing lines for the pattern repeats through points S. (If you imagine the small section of the curve at S is straight, then the dividing line crosses the line at right angles. The long marks on a ruler every inch or centimetre meet its drawing edge at right angles, so if when drawing a dividing line, an inch or centimetre mark on a transparent ruler is lined up along the curve the angle should be about right.) However, since the methods described for drawing the ellipse and dividing lines are not mathematically exact, some adjustment may be necessary. Using a flexi-curve or French curves draw the diagonals across the pattern repeats crossing on the centre line at T.

Count the number of points along the length of the pattern repeat R on squared paper. Mark these points along the inner and outer curves for each pattern repeat along the elliptical band (figure 185). Since the headside of my pattern was a series of fans the curves that produce the ground needed only to be drawn as far as the inner boundary of the fans so the divisions were marked here instead. Curves were drawn connecting the two sets of points with all the curves kept as evenly spaced as possible. Sometimes it is easier to sketch them freehand than using drawing aids. This method produces a grid with pattern repeats having the same number of points along and across each section. My pattern was slightly wider so the curves were extended along the inner edge to find the positions of the footside points F. The low points U between the fans were found by measuring. The curves of the fans were drawn as usual and lines drawn for the central division of the fans. The pricking was made from the grid, omitting points as required (figure 186).

Take care when choosing the thread. The original pattern is a guide if you have kept strictly to its grid size. The majority of this pattern was worked in DMC Retors d'Alsace No. 30 with DMC Perle No. 8 for the gimp. However since the 'spreading' effect is most noticeable in the fans the worker for these were wound double.

Figure 187.
An elliptical edging made on
pricking figure 184 using DMC
Retors d'Alsace No.30 and 50 gimps
DMC Perle No.8

132

13.
Making a Pricking

Parchment for prickings is, unfortunately, very difficult to obtain but glazed manilla card, produced for electrical insulation, is a suitable substitute and is available from most lace equipment suppliers. It is more difficult to prick than softer card, e.g. cornflakes packets, but the holes will not enlarge and the stiffness of the card acts as a support, holding the pins in position.

The pricking card should be placed on a flat surface for pricking, not a curved pillow. Four layers of corrugated cardboard, secured together with cellophane tape, make a satisfactory board on which to prick. Fix the draft to the card using cellophane tape, staples (rough side up), Blu Tack or pins, and the card to the pricking board using a pin at each corner. The needle in the pricker should have the same diameter as the pins that are to be used for making the lace; too small a hole results in the bending of pins (which happens all too frequently, even when the holes are sufficiently large). Too large a hole results in lack of support for the pins and consequently lack of accuracy of the finished lace. The tip of the needle should protrude only about 6mm (1/4in) from the pricker. A longer point will break more easily. If a 'sharps' needle is used in a pricker breakages can sometimes be reduced by using a shorter needle e.g. a 'between' or by cutting the needle in half using pliers (take care as the pieces can fly when the needle is cut). Using two pairs of pliers and breaking the needle by bending it is often safer than cutting. The needle portion of the pricker should be pushed right into the card at every hole. Stabbing the needle into beeswax occasionally will add sufficient lubrication to make pricking easier. The chubby, bulbous prickers are more comfortable to use than the narrow, pencil-like ones generally available. Keep the pricker as vertical as possible when working.

With the exception of the footside, always prick the holes in the order in which they will probably be worked. When pricking the footside make two holes several inches apart, set up pins in these holes and slide a ruler tightly against them. Prick the remaining footside holes with the pricker resting against the ruler.

Once the pricking has been completed leave the pins that hold the card and paper together and hold the pair up to the light, or turn over. Examine either the points of light or the bumps and look for blank areas where points have been missed. Replace the pattern and card on the board and prick 'the ones that got away'. Various lines and squiggles can be seen on many old patterns. Some symbols are widely used, others are individual. Draw guidelines of your choice to help you make good lace. I frequently use different colours when there is more than one gimp thread following tortuous routes with frequent crossings. Traditionally, indian ink was used for drawing guidelines but very fine felt tip pens work well on pricking card. When purchasing a pen take a small piece of card for testing and keep the pen for marking pricking card only. Pens in general use often end up with tips like paintbrushes. Always draw the lines in pencil first. Trace over them in pen and, when the pen lines are dry, erase the pencil marks which may dirty the lace. Unwanted holes should be ringed ⊙ to prevent their use. If a pattern is very complicated 'non-smudge' carbon paper can be slipped between the pattern draft and the card after the holes have been pricked. Draw over the guidelines with a stiletto or ball-point pen to transfer them to the card. These lines are not always sufficiently dark but a felt tip pen will remedy this. Again an eraser can be used to clean up after the pen lines are dry but I have not experienced any dirtying caused by this carbon paper.

An alternative is to cover the white pattern with blue or green adhesive book-covering film a little larger than the pattern and use the overhang to attach both to the card. Judicious rubbing with steel wool (not the soapy kind) will remove shine and reflections. The pattern should be fully

Figure 188.
A *repeating pattern*

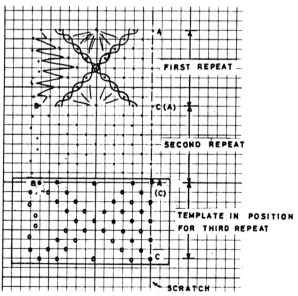

134

pricked before commencing lacemaking. Always have a medium coloured pricking if white or pale thread is used and mark with black or a dark pen. When black or dark thread is to be used the card should have a pastel coloured surface (cover with pale paper) and use a light coloured pen. Red shows up well against pale paper and black thread.

Figure 190.

Dovetailing two pattern pieces.

Fitting the first section to the second

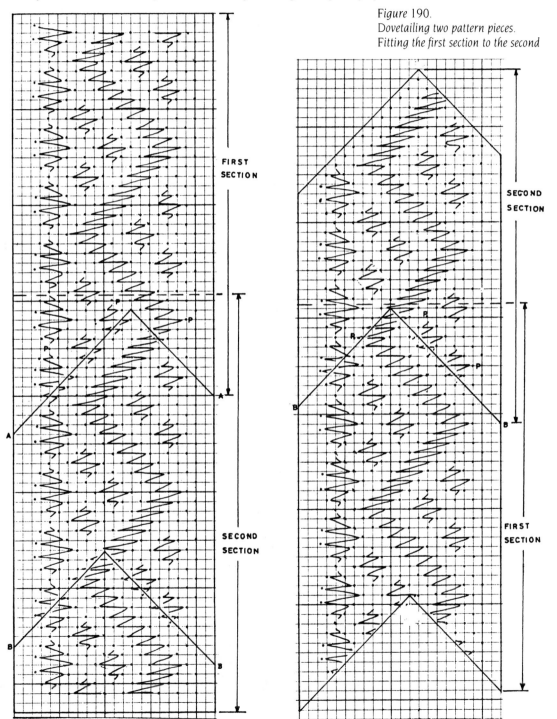

FIRST
SECTION

SECOND
SECTION

SECOND
SECTION

FIRST
SECTION

REPEATING PATTERN

If a long pricking is to be made prick one pattern repeat plus one line of holes on transparent acetate and make a scratch line on the card to show the footside position. Place the transparent template on the card with the footside holes along the scratch and insert pins through the card at both ends of the template footside (points *A* and *C*). Prick the other holes in the template. *Remove the template and place the pin through its top footside hole *A* in to the lowest one in the card *C*. Rotate the template until its footside covers the scratch and its top line of holes covers the lowest line in the pricking card. Place a pin at the other end of the matched line of holes *B* and at the lower end of the template footside *C*. Prick the pattern. Repeat from * as required (figure 188).

DOVETAILING

If a long piece of lace is to be made on a flat-topped pillow two dovetailing pieces of pattern may be used. Draft the pattern pieces a little longer than required. Cut a 'V' *A-A* at the lower end of the first section so that the cut does not touch any of the pinholes (figures 189). Place the cut end *A-A* of the first section over the beginning of the second section and insert pins through several matching pinholes *P*; choose easily recognisable positions, e.g. spider centres, the point of a diamond, etc. Then using a pricker or berry pin scratch the second section along edge *A-A* of the first section. Remove the pins and carefully cut along the scratch line. Place the pattern pieces end to end and check that no lumps or bumps left along the cutting lines are spoiling the 'fit' of the pieces. Cut a 'V' *B-B* at the other end of the second section, place this cut end *B-B* over the beginning of the first section matching the pinholes *P* (figure 190) scratch the first section along *B-B* and cut. Place the two pieces end to end as before and check for 'fit'. Make the lace working from one pattern piece to the next, moving the work up the pillow as necessary.

FITTING A PATTERN ON A ROLLER

When using a pillow with a roller, e.g. a French- or Swedish-style pillow, make the pattern in one piece so that it will reach round the roller and overlap by one pattern repeat then dovetail the ends (figure 191). If necessary improve the fit of the pattern round a stuffed roller by placing a piece of thick open-weave woollen material under the pattern. Thin polystyrene sheet (the type used under wallpaper) should be used for packing polystyrene pillows. Use sufficient packing to make the pattern a good fit. There should be at least 6mm (¼in) clearance between the roller and its box to accommodate the packing.

Figure 191
Packing a roller to make the pattern fit

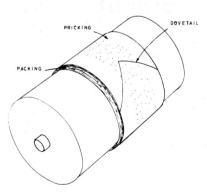

APPENDIX – GRIDS

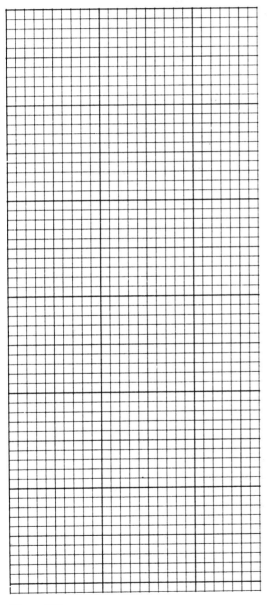

Figure 192
$^1/_{10}in$

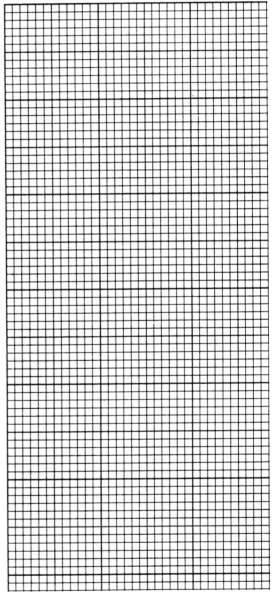

Figure 193
$^1/_{12}in$

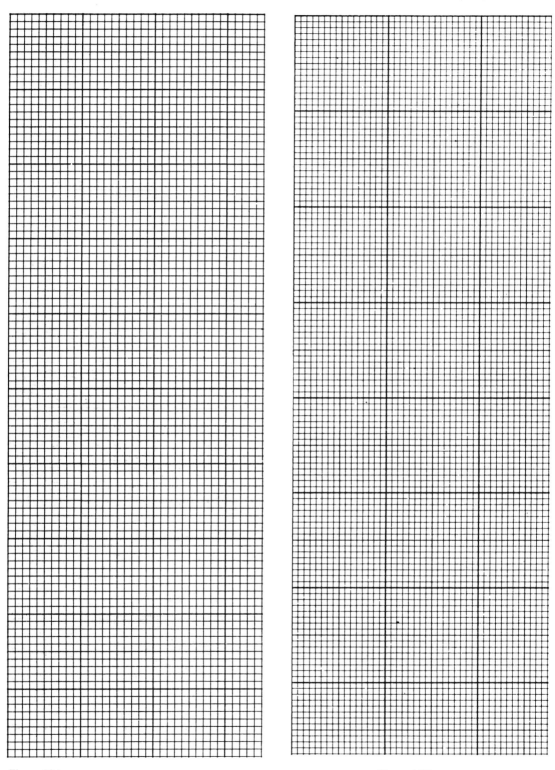

Figure 194
2mm

Figure 195
¹/₁₆in

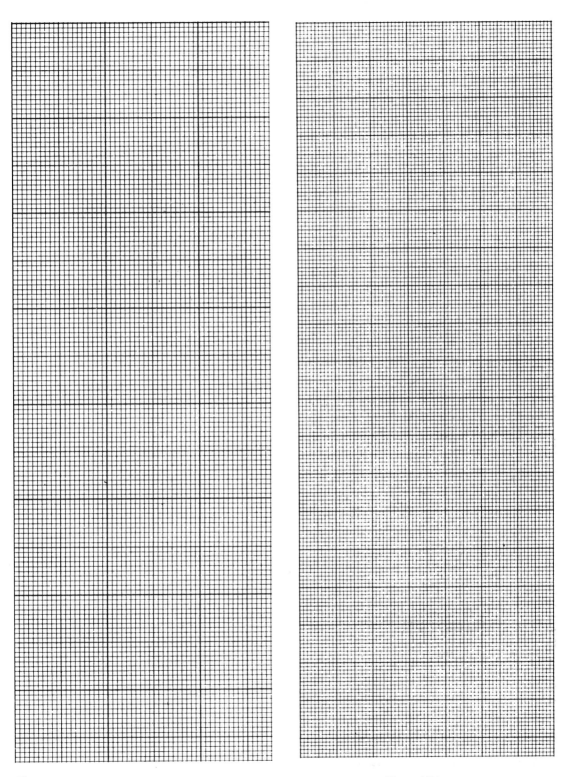

Figure 196.
$^1/_{20}$in

Figure 197.
$1mm$

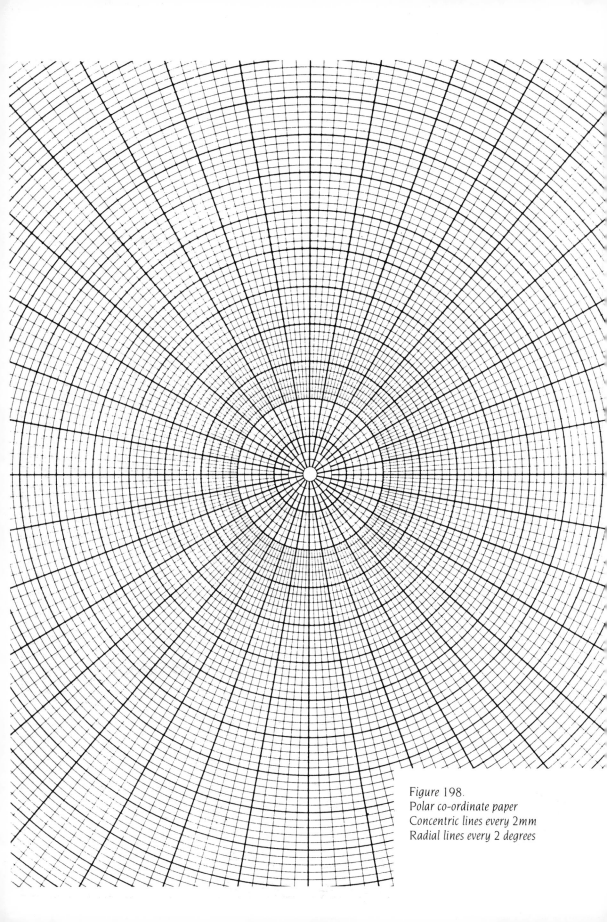

Figure 198.
Polar co-ordinate paper
Concentric lines every 2mm
Radial lines every 2 degrees

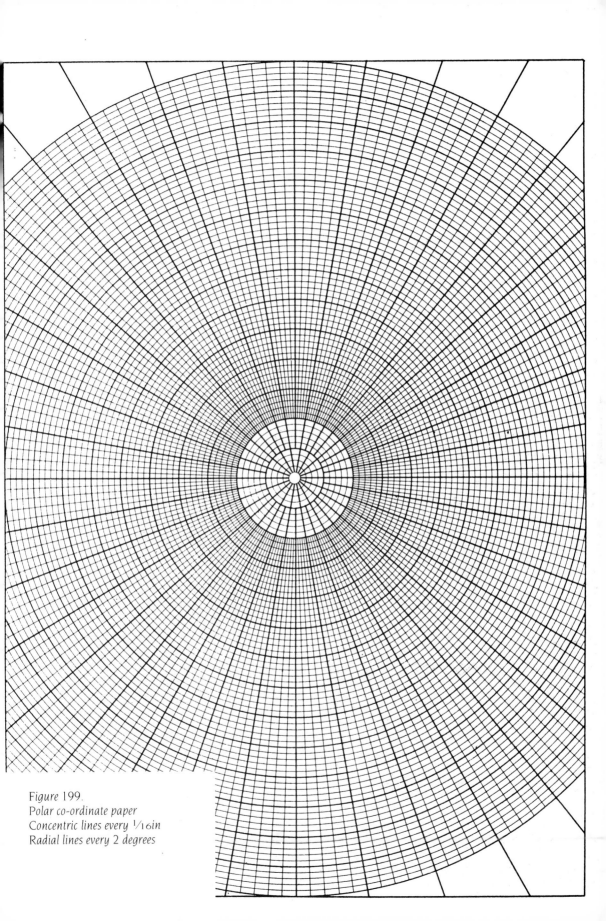

Figure 199.
Polar co-ordinate paper
Concentric lines every ¹/₁₆in
Radial lines every 2 degrees

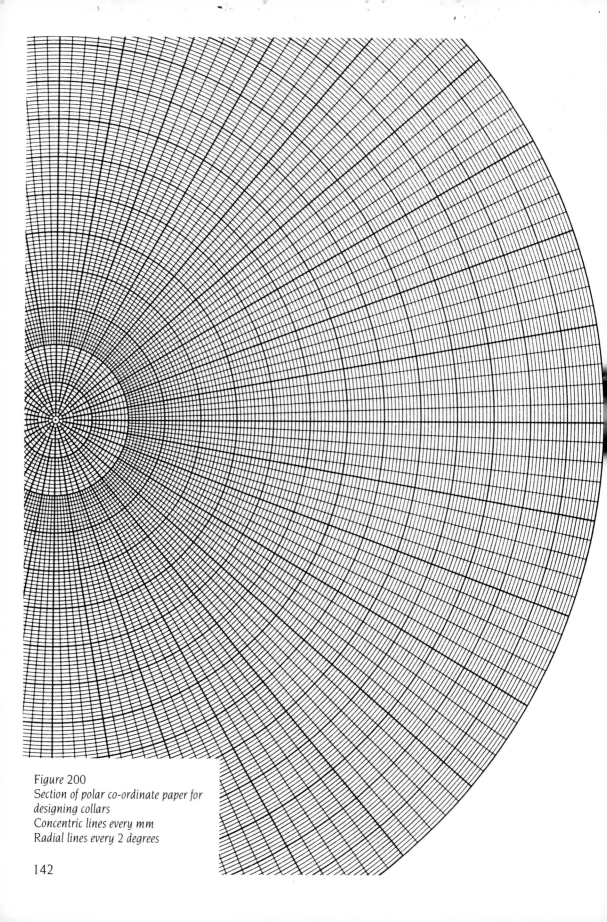

Figure 200
Section of polar co-ordinate paper for
designing collars
Concentric lines every mm
Radial lines every 2 degrees

142

SUPPLIERS

FURTHER READING

General lacemaking supplies, graph paper and radius aids

A. Sells
'Lane Cove'
49 Pedley Lane
Clifton
Shefford
Bedfordshire

General lacemaking supplies, graph paper and radius aids

D.J. Hornsby
149 High Street
Burton Latimer
Kettering
Northants
NN15 5RL

Silk thread

E. & V. Piper
'Silverlea'
Glemsford
Suffolk
CO10 7RS

Office supplies – graph papers, drawing instruments etc.

Hussey & Greaves Ltd
26 Baddow Road
Chelmsford
Essex
CM2 0HJ

Wooden items – bobbins, boxes etc. Chubby prickers made to order for those suffering from arthritis. Highly recommended for everyone.

Richard Gravestock
Lanterns
104 New Road
Haslingfield
Cambridge
C83 7LP

Torchon pattern drafting and lacemaking

Cook, Bridget, and Stott, Geraldine, *The Book of Bobbin Lace Stitches*, Batsford

DMC Deutelle aux Fuseaux. I

Dye, Gilian, *Beginning Bobbin Lace*, Dryad Press

Fisher, Jennifer, *Torchon Lace for Today*, Dryad Press

Olsson, Inga-Lisa, *Knypplerskan*, I and II, Holmqvists

Kortelahti, Eeva-Lissa, *Bobbin Lace*

Maidment, Margaret, *Hand-made Bobbin Lacework*, Batsford

Mincott, E., and Marriage, M., *Pillow Lace*, Minet

Nottingham, Pamela, *Technique of Bobbin Lace*, Batsford

Nottingham, Pamela, *Technique of Torchon Lace*, Batsford

Other lacemaking techniques

Cook, Bridget, and Stott, Geraldine, *Introduction to Bobbin Lace Patterns*, Batsford

Dye, Gilian, *Bobbin Lace Braid*, Batsford

Lovesey, Nenia, and Barley, Catherine, *Venetian Gros Point Lace*, Dryad Press

Maidens, Ena, *Technique of Irish Crochet Lace*, Batsford

Withers, Jean, *Mounting and Using Lace*, Dryad Press

INDEX

acetate sheet 9 (*see also* template)
adapting patterns 70

basic fan 11, 13, 49, 85, 113
bookmark 93, 95
borders 36, 43
brooch motif 85

centre seam 89
changing scale 62
circular edging 113, 126
circular mat 117
collar 104, 120
compound spiders 56, 62, 84, 98, 120
copying patterns 7, 47
corner 13, 25, 29, 33, 55, 60, 71
coronet fan 32, 44, 84, 90
cucumber foot 120
curves, plotting 13, 27, 30, 32, 43

decorated fans and borders 43, 90, 102
designing 16, 97, 104, 106, 120
diamonds 48, 51, 61, 64, 72, 76, 88, 95, 122
double fan 18, 20, 21, 22, 76
dovetailing pattern 136

Edwardian lady picture 106
ellipse 126 (*see also* oval edging)
extended corner 80

fan (*see* basic fan)
fan leaf 122
fans, summary 22
feather 30
fillings 60, 72, 106, 110
fir tree fan (*see* Spanish fan)
flexicurve 10, 129
footside 12, 62, 133

freestyle pieces 106, 122
French curves 9, 10, 13, 128
French fan 34, 52, 64, 72, 83, 119
fringe 45

German spider border 40
gimps 59, 78, 103, 116
graph paper 9, 62, 137
guidelines 13, 50, 134

hearts 53, 72, 87
heart-shaped fan 18, 20, 21, 47

insertion 93, 96, 97
inward-curving fan 18, 19, 20, 61, 86
inward-facing corner 76
items made in several pieces 97

large pea border 39, 78

masking 25
mat (*see* square or rectangular mat)
mirror 70, 73, 76, 81, 83, 84, 86, 90, 94, 98
mock footside 79

non-reversing corner 74

oval edging 126 (*see also* ellipse)

paperweight motif 83
Paris fan (*see* French fan)
pea border 37, 56, 74
peaked scallop 43, 123
photocopies 7, 134
plain border 36, 51, 59, 82
plain fan (*see* basic fan)
plaited decoration 45, 90
points along a curve (*see* curve)

pricker 133
pricking
    board 133
    card 133
    making a 133

radius aid 9, 10, 13
rectangular mat 89
repeating pattern 136
roller, pattern for 136
rose ground 48, 122, 125
runner end 79

scallop border 43, 123
scallop fan (*see* coronet fan)
seam (*see* centre seam)
shell fan (*see* French fan)
side reverse 72
simple fan (*see* basic fan)
Spanish fan 23, 45, 64, 94, 127, 130
    variation 27, 50, 94, 116
spiders 56, 61, 72, 76, 83, 84, 90, 94, 102
    (*see also* compound spiders)
square mat 88, 97
straight-edged fan 18, 19, 54

tablecloth 97
tallies 56, 60, 112
template 13, 25, 33
thread chart 64
toadstool picture 110
torchon ground 12, 62, 114, 118
transparent template (*see* template)
triangles 48, 49, 51, 64, 82, 119
trail 53, 56, 60, 72, 76, 94, 96
trail edge 18, 21, 22, 55, 120

wide circular edging 117